W9-ARN-496

WRIGLEY FIELD
HOME OF
CHICAGO CUBS
CHICAGO'S #1
BARBECUE SAUCE

Fodor's CITYPACK

CHICAGO'S
25 BEST

WITH FULL-SIZE
FOLDOUT MAP

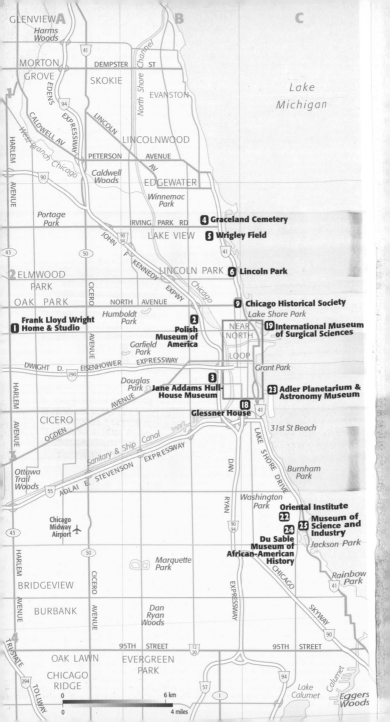

GLENVIEW **A** **B** **C**

Harms
Woods

MORTON
GROVE

SKOKIE

DEMPSTER ST

Evanston

Lake
Michigan

LINCOLNWOOD

PETERSON AVENUE

EDGEWATER

Winnemac
Park

IRVING PARK RD **4** **Graceland Cemetery**

LAKE VIEW **5** **Wrigley Field**

LINCOLN PARK **6** **Lincoln Park**

9 **Chicago Historical Society**

Lake Shore Park

NEAR
NORTH

19 **International Museum
of Surgical Sciences**

2
**Polish
Museum of
America**

ELMWOOD
PARK

OAK PARK

NORTH AVENUE

Humboldt
Park

1 **Frank Lloyd Wright
Home & Studio**

Garfield
Park

DWIGHT D. EISENHOWER EXPRESSWAY

LOOP

Grant Park

Douglas
Park

3
**Jane Addams Hull-
House Museum**

CICERO

OGDEN

23 **Adler Planetarium &
Astronomy Museum**

18
Glessner House

31st St Beach

Sanitary & Ship Canal

Ottawa
Trail
Woods

ADLAI E. STEVENSON EXPRESSWAY

Burnham
Park

Washington
Park

22 **Oriental Institute**

Chicago
Midway
Airport

25 **Museum of
Science and
Industry**

24
**Du Sable
Museum of
African-American
History**

Jackson Park

Marquette
Park

BRIDGEVIEW

Rainbow
Park

BURBANK

Dan
Ryan
Woods

95TH STREET

95TH STREET

OAK LAWN

EVERGREEN
PARK

CHICAGO
RIDGE

Lake
Calumet

Eggers
Woods

0   6 km
0   4 miles

Top 25 locator map
(continues on inside
back cover)
←

Fodor's CITYPACK
CHICAGO'S 25 BEST

by Mick Sinclair

Fodor's Travel Publications
New York • Toronto •
London • Sydney • Auckland
www.fodors.com

About This Book

KEY TO SYMBOLS

➕ Map reference to the accompanying fold-out map and Top 25 locator map

✉ Address

☎ Telephone number

🕐 Opening/closing times

🍴 Restaurant or café on premises or nearby

🚆 Nearest railroad station

Ⓜ Nearest subway (tube) station

🚍 Nearest bus route

🚢 Nearest riverboat or ferry stop

♿ Facilities for visitors with disabilities

✋ Admission charges: Expensive (over $13), Moderate ($7–$13) and Inexpensive (under $7)

↔ Other nearby places of interest

❓ Other practical information

▶ Indicates the page where you will find a fuller description

ℹ Tourist information

ORGANIZATION

This guide is divided into six chapters:

- Planning Ahead, Getting There
- Living Chicago—Chicago Now, Chicago Then, Time to Shop, Out and About, Walks, Chicago by Night
- Chicago's Top 25 Sights
- Chicago's Best—best of the rest
- Where To—detailed listings of restaurants, hotels, shops and nightlife
- Travel Facts—practical information

In addition, easy-to-read side panels provide extra facts and snippets, highlights of places to visit and invaluable practical advice.

The colors of the tabs on the page corners match the colors of the triangles aligned with the chapter names on the contents page opposite.

MAPS

The fold-out map in the wallet at the back of this book is a comprehensive street plan of Chicago. The first (or only) grid reference given for each attraction refers to this map. **The Top 25 locator map** found on the inside front and back covers of the book itself is for quick reference. It shows the Top 25 Sights, described on pages 26–50, which are clearly plotted by number (**1**–**25**, not page number) across the city. The second map reference given for the Top 25 Sights refers to this map.

Contents

Planning Ahead

WHEN TO GO

June, July and August are the busiest months, but the weather can be tryingly hot. May, September and October are better months to visit, with fewer crowds and warm but less extreme weather. Events and festivals take place year-round. Major conventions in August, September and October cause hotel space to be scarce.

TIME

Chicago is one hour behind New York, two hours ahead of Los Angeles and six hours behind the UK.

AVERAGE DAILY MAXIMUM TEMPERATURES

JAN	FEB	MAR	APR	MAY	JUN	JUL	AUG	SEP	OCT	NOV	DEC
22°F	26°F	37°F	49°F	59°F	69°F	74°F	72°F	65°F	53°F	40°F	27°F
-6°C	-3°C	3°C	9°C	15°C	21°C	23°C	22°C	18°C	12°C	4°C	-3°C

Spring (mid-March to May) Very changeable; sometimes blizzards, sometimes sun but generally mild.

Summer (June to mid-September) Varies from warm to very hot, sometimes uncomfortably so with high humidity.

Autumn (mid-September to October) Though changeable it is often mild with sunny days.

Winter (November to mid-March) Often very cold with heavy snow and strong winds. Winds can be strong any time and particularly cold when, usually in winter, they come from the north.

WHAT'S ON

January/February *Chinese New Year*: In Chinatown.

March *St. Patrick's Day*: The whole city, including the Chicago River, turns green, and there's a parade through the Loop.

April *Spring flower shows*: Lincoln Park and Garfield Park conservatories.

May *Polish Constitution Day* (7 May): Chicago's Polish Americans celebrate with a parade and events focusing on Polish culture.

Wright Plus: See inside Oak Park homes designed by Frank Lloyd Wright.

June *Chicago Blues Festival*: Local and international artists perform for massive audiences in Grant Park.

Printer's Row Book Fair: Used-book shops offer bargains and host events.

Chicago Gospel Festival: Gospel music in Grant Park.

July *Taste of Chicago*: a feeding frenzy; in the 11 days leading up to 4 July, thousands sample dishes from city restaurants.

Independence Day (4 Jul): Special events such as fireworks displays, the largest taking place in Grant Park.

August *Ravinia Festival* (mid-Jun to Labor Day): Two months of the Chicago Symphony Orchestra, plays and other cultural events, with picnicking on the lawns.

Chicago Air & Water Show: Spectacular stunts performed off North Avenue Beach.

September *Chicago Jazz Festival*: Jazz stars headline free concerts in Grant Park.

October *Chicago Marathon*.

November/December *Festival of Lights*: 30,000 lights illuminate the Magnificent Mile.

CHICAGO ONLINE

www.ci.chi.il.us
The city government website, Chicagoans use this to pay their bills and make complaints, but it holds plenty of interest to visitors.

www.choosechicago.com
Part of the above, but aimed more squarely at visitors. Most sections comprise links to other organizations, but it's a good start point, annual events and cultural activities.

www.chicagotribune.com
The online version of Chicago's biggest circulation daily newspaper and requires (free) registration. Its listings sister site, metromix (see below), is free and does not require registration.

www.suntimes.com
The online version of Chicago's tabloid daily newspaper, with full access to news and feature stories, plus sports and, if you should want it, access to its advertisements.

www.chicagoreader.com
The website of the city's long-established alternative weekly newspaper, the *Chicago Reader*, with a different slant on city affairs and its own recommendations for entertainment and culture.

www.newcitychicago.com
A more recent alternative weekly, *New City Chicago* is slicker and snappier in style than the *Reader*, but sometimes less satisfying.

www.metromix.com
Offshoot of the *Chicago Tribune* with informative listings, covering events, museums, dining, nightlife and more.

www.urchicago.com
Opinionated takes on the Chicago clubbing scene and much more about the city from a late-night perspective.

GOOD TRAVEL SITES

www.fodors.com
A complete travel-planning site. Research prices and the weather; reserve air tickets, cars and rooms; ask questions (and get answers) from fellow visitors; and find links to other sites.

www.transitchicago.com
The website of the Chicago Transit Authority explains all there is to know about using the city's buses and El trains, the fares and ticket types, with route maps that can be downloaded and lots more.

CYBERCAFÉS

Cyberia
Popular Wicker Park hangout offering a limited selection of drinks and snacks.
Off map ✉ 1331 N Ashland Avenue
☎ 773/384–4881
🕐 Mon–Thu 9–9, Fri, Sat 9am–10pm, Sun 10am–7pm 💲 $5 per hr

Screenz Digital Universe
Broadband connections and screened-off workstations with all the appropriate software.
F1 ✉ 2717 N Clark Street ☎ 773/244–1633
🕐 Daily 10am–midnight
💲 $10–$12 per hr

Getting There

ENTRY REQUIREMENTS

UK citizens require a machine readable passport, valid for at least six months. Passports issued on or after 26 October 2004 must include a biometric identifier; UK passports already issued will still qualify for visa-free travel, as will those of other countries in the visa-waiver scheme. Check the current situation before you leave (US Embassy visa information ☎ 0891 200-2900; www.usembassy.org).

MONEY

Dollar bills (notes) come in denominations of $1, $5, $10, $20, $50 and $100; coins are 25¢ (a quarter), 10¢ (a dime), 5¢ (a nickel) and 1¢ (a penny).

$5

$10

$50

$100

ARRIVING

Chicago's O'Hare International Airport is 17 miles (27km) northwest of the Loop and handles all international flights and most domestic flights. Midway Airport, 8 miles (13km) southwest of the Loop, is a quieter alternative for domestic flights.

FROM O'HARE INTERNATIONAL AIRPORT

For information on O'Hare International Airport ☎ 773/686–2000; www.ohare.com.

Continental Air Transport (☎ 312/454–800 or 800/654–7871; www.airportexpress.com) runs minibuses between O'Hare and the Loop every five minutes 6am–11.30pm (fare $17.50; journey time 45 minutes). Pick them up from outside the arrivals terminal.

Chicago Transit Authority (☎ 888/YOUR–CTA; www.transitchicago.com) operates Blue Line trains between O'Hare and the Loop (24 hours; journey time 45 minutes; fare $1.75). Follow the signs from the arrivals hall to the station.

However, it is safer to take a taxi late at night from either airport. Taxis wait outside the arrivals terminal and the fare to the Loop or nearby hotels is about $35–$40.

ARRIVING AT MIDWAY AIRPORT

For information about Midway Airport ☎ 773/838–0600; www.ohare.com/midway/home.asp.

Continental Air Transport (► above) runs minibuses to the Loop every 15 minutes

6am–10.30pm (fare around $6; journey time 30 minutes). Pick them up from outside Door 3.
Chicago Transit Authority (► 6) runs Orange Line trains to the Loop from 3.55am–12.55am, slightly later/earlier on weekends and holidays, (fare $1.75; journey time 30 minutes).
Taxis wait at the arrivals terminal. The fare to the Loop or nearby hotels is approximately $25.

ARRIVING BY BUS
Greyhound buses (☎ 800/229–9424; 312/408–5800; www.greyhound.com) arrive at 630 W. Harrison Street, six blocks southwest of the Loop.

ARRIVING BY TRAIN
Amtrak trains use Chicago's Union Station, junction of W. Adams and S. Canal streets, two blocks west of the Loop. Information ☎ 800/872–7245; 312/655–2111; www.amtrak.com

ARRIVING BY CAR
Chicago has good Interstate access: I-80 and I-90 are the major east–west routes; I-55 and I-57 arrive from the south. I-94 runs through the city linking the north and south suburbs. To reach the Loop from O'Hare airport use I-90/94. From Midway airport take I-55, linking with the northbound I-90/94 for the Loop. These journeys take 45–90 minutes and 30–60 minutes respectively. Avoid the rush hours, 7–9am and 4–7pm.

GETTING AROUND
Much of Chicago can be explored on foot. To travel between neighborhoods use the network of buses and El (elevated) trains, which travel above and below ground. El trains operate 24-hours a day, but using trains or buses late at night can be dangerous. Best value over many journeys are the Visitor Pass tickets valid for 1–5 days (cost $5–$18). Buy them from the airport CTA stations, from major museums and the Visitor Information (for information ☎ 1-888-YOURCTA). Tokens, cash and multi-use plastic cards can also be used. Taxis wait outside hotels, conference halls and major El stations, or can be hailed. For more information on getting around ► 91.

INSURANCE
It is vital to have cover for medical expenses, as well as theft, baggage loss, trip cancellation and accidents. Check your insurance coverage and buy a supplementary policy as needed.

DRIVING IN CHICAGO
Driving in the city is stressful: use public transportation. Many hotels have parking lots, otherwise overnight parking is difficult and very costly. During the day, street parking is often limited to two hours; spaces in the Loop are near impossible to find.

VISITORS WITH DISABILITIES
Legislation aimed at improving access for visitors with disabilities in Chicago means that all recently built structures have to provide disabled access; the newer they are, the stricter the rules. Many older buildings, including most hotels, have been converted to ensure they comply. Both airports are accessible, as are many CTA buses and El stations. For details www.transitchicago.com/maps/accessible.html

Living
Chicago

Chicago Now

Above: *The Chicago skyline at night*
Right: *Monument with Standing Beast (1985), the controversial Dubuffet sculpture in front of the James R. Thompson Center*

Chicago could hardly announce itself in bolder style. Whether approached by road, rail or air, the city rises with glamour and panache above the vast expanse of Lake Michigan to the east and the flatlands that stretch for hundreds of miles to the west. Chicago's unmistakable skyline is the calling card of a city that grew fast and grew rich on trade, the commercial crossroads that connected the populace of the American east to

NEIGHBORHOODS

- The Loop, the business-oriented downtown area around which El train and bus routes converge, bordered to the north and west by the Chicago River, is at the heart of Chicago's 77 neighborhoods. Most of the other key areas for visitors are to the north. In geographical order, they are the Magnificent Mile and the River North and River West areas, the Gold Coast and the Old Town, adjacent to Lake Michigan and just inland respectively; Lincoln Park/DePaul, with Wicker Park and Bucktown farther west; and Wrigleyville and Lake View. Immediately south of the Loop is the aptly named South Loop, while the regions of note beyond are Chinatown and Hyde Park/Kenwood.

MIKE DITKA

• Mike Ditka's coaching of the Chicago Bears led to Superbowl success in 1986 and the team's eleven-year domination of the NFL. Pennsylvania born Ditka is praised on the Bears website as a 'bull-necked, broad-shouldered, hard-nosed competitor', a description that for some might be the very embodiment of Chicago attitude but for others represents an image Chicago wants to live down.

the farms of the Midwest and became a financial linchpin for the nation's heartland.

Yet while the city took shape in the 19th-century and matured during the 20th, Chicago is eagerly looking to reshape itself for the 21st century. As its regional business importance remains undiminished, there is a growing emphasis on making Chicago a great place to be in, rather than just to work in. 'Building a better Chicago' is the current buzz-phrase (even though the idea has been the ethos of every Chicago politician seeking office for decades) and one that is beginning to reap rewards.

While many improvements, in schools, housing and in other fields, might be out of sight of visitors, environmental improvements are anything but hidden. Most spectacular of all is the major addition to Grant Park named (optimistically, since much remains under construction) Millennium Park, the features of which include a zigzagging auditorium from renowned architect Frank Gehry and a 100-ton reflective sculpture resembling, perhaps, a futuristic Chicago hot dog, by the globally acclaimed Anish Kapoor.

Above: *Modern sculpture on the edge of Grant Park*
Above right: *Lakeside Chicago*

On a smaller scale, the Riverwalk is in the process of making the Chicago River a recreational as well as a geographical feature of the city, forming a waterside path running parallel to Wabash Avenue that enables walkers, joggers and cyclists to connect with the long-established lakeside trail and enjoy cafés, artworks and other items of interest along the route.

Another new park may yet appear from the controversial midnight bulldozing during 2003 of the runway at Meigs Field, a small airport used by private planes. Instigating the action, Mayor Daley claimed it was necessary to reduce risk of airborne terrorist attack while also reclaiming the airport's lakeside area for the people of Chicago. Increasingly, however, it is the people rather than the mayor who are seeking to force the issue and ensure a park actually does emerge from the rubble.

Such people power is indeed a feature of Chicago, where community and neighborhood organizations are a notable aspect of city life and the population is accustomed to organizing itself and vocally making demands of those who

OPRAH WINFREY

• It was in Chicago that Oprah Winfrey made her name. Born in Mississippi, she arrived in Chicago in 1984 and turned a moribund morning TV chat show into the hugely successful *Oprah Winfrey Show*. Frank discussions of emotional and social issues became a sensation and made Winfrey a worldwide star.

12

govern, aware and critical of the famously (some might say infamously) tight-knit relations between the city's big business, politics and the unions.

Above: *Volley ball is played on the mile- (2-km) long North Avenue Beach*

Frank Gehry's contribution might be seen as part of the city's tradition of cutting-edge urban design that stretches back to Daniel Burnham and Louis Sullivan, who helped reshape Chicago after a devastating fire in 1871. The reputation that Chicago gained as a city of modern architecture was furthered by Frank Lloyd Wright and particularly strengthened in the 1950s and 1960s by Mies van der Rohe, whose groundbreaking additions the to city included Marina City, his

MICHAEL JORDAN

• A major contribution to the success of the Chicago Bulls, Michael Jordan is among basketball's all-time greats. Born in Brooklyn, Jordan joined the Bulls in 1984 and went on to top the NBA scoring charts for seven consecutive seasons. After leading the Bulls to six world championships, he retired in 1999 but made several comeback attempts.

NAMING CHICAGO

• Chicago takes its name from 'Checagou' (pronounced 'Cha-Ah-Gou-Ah') a word of the native Potawatomi people. The word means 'rotting onions' or 'skunk' and is regarded as a reference either to the smell of the rotting onions that once covered the marshland on which the city of Chicago grew, or a term to describe the onions themselves.

13

Above: *Frank Lloyd Wright's studio*
Above right: *Oak Street Beach*

glass-and-steel Lake Shore Drive apartments and the campus of the Illinois Institute of Technology.

Architecture alone can fill a visit to Chicago but the city can also claim the rare distinction of offering world-class art and history collections (with the Art Institute and Chicago Historical Society respectively), and the world's most complete *Tyrannosaurus rex* (at the Field Museum of Natural History), while also enjoying a reputation for distinctive hot dogs and deep-pan pizza.

Chicago shopping, too, fills a broad horizon: from the prestigious malls of the Magnificent Mile to the funky one-of-a-kind shops of Lake View and

TRIVIA

- Chicago's William Wrigley Jr. is the world's biggest chewing gum manufacturer.
- Chicago is the third-largest city in the US and has a population of 2.9 million.
- Chicago has 15 miles (24km) of beach, 18 miles (29km) of lakefront bicycle paths and 552 parks.
- Chicago's Lyon & Healy is the world's oldest maker of standing string harps.

SAMMY SOSA

- Sammy Sosa crossed Chicago from the White Sox to the Cubs in 1992 and six years later made baseball history by hitting a record number of home runs in a season. Sensation turned to suspicion during a game in 2002 when Sosa was discovered to be using an illegal corked bat.

Wrigleyville, via a plethora of independent book-stores, antiques outlets and art galleries. Chicago can also be enjoyed without expenditure of any kind: 15 miles (24km) of beaches belie the fact that the nearest ocean is nearly a thousand miles (1,609km) away, and a nine-month-long program of events takes place for free in the city's parks and open spaces.

Yet the real buzz of Chicago is simply walking the streets and exploring a few of the city's 77 neigh-borhoods, each with its own looks and atmosphere. Many retain the mark of the ethnic group that first settled them (and in some cases remain prevalent). Irish, Italians, Poles and Germans were among the early arrivals from Europe; Latin Americans and Asians also feature strongly in the city's racial mix, as do African-Americans who have contributed greatly to Chicago's identity and, among other achieve-ments, helped make it a place of pilgrimage for the world's blues and jazz fans.

Despite the difficulties that beset any major city, Chicago's future direction, like its world-famous buildings, seems determinedly upward.

Above: *Joán Miró's massive sculpture,* Chicago *in The Loop, downtown*
Above left: *View along La Salle Street*

CHICAGO HOT AND COLD

● Chicago's highest temperature was recorded at Midway Airport on 13 July, 1995, when the thermometer reached 106°F (41°C), although the official weather station at O'Hare airport noted a mere 104°F (40°C). By contrast, the city's coldest day was 20 January, 1985 when the mercury dropped to -27°F (-33°C) degrees.

15

Chicago Then

VISIT
CLARKE HOUSE
1836
CHICAGO'S OLDEST BUILDING
TURN RIGHT ON 18th STREET TO THE
PRAIRIE AVENUE HISTORIC DISTRICT TOUR CENTER

THE HAYMARKET RIOT

Heavy-handed police tactics in a series of labor disputes prompted a group of German-born anarchists to organize a protest rally on 4 May 1886, in Haymarket Square. A bomb thrown from the crowd exploded among the police lines; the explosion and the police use of firearms killed seven people and wounded 150. Seven anarchists received death sentences. In 1893, a full pardon was granted to three imprisoned anarchists, due to the lack of evidence linking any anarchists to the bomb.

WINDY CITY

In 1893 Chicago hosted the World's Columbian Exposition. The hyperbole of business leaders caused one journalist to describe Chicago as "the windy city," an enduring epithet.

1673 Jacques Marquette and Louis Joliet discover the 1.5 mile (2.4km) Native-American portage trail linking the Mississippi River and the Great Lakes—the site of future Chicago.

1779–81 Trapper and trader Jean-Baptiste Point du Sable, a Haitian, becomes the first non-native settler.

1812 Fort Dearborn, one of several forts protecting trade routes, is attacked by Native Americans.

1830 Chicago is selected as the site of a canal linking the Great Lakes and the Mississippi.

1870 Chicago's population reaches 30,000. Many arrivals are Irish, who find work building the railways.

1871 The Great Fire kills 250 people.

1894 A strike at the Pullman rail company unites black and white workers for the first time.

1906 Upton Sinclair's novel *The Jungle* focuses national attention on the conditions endured by workers in the notorious Union Stockyards.

1908 Chicago Cubs win baseball's World Series for a second successive year.

1914   With World War I, Chicago's black population increases further, as African-Americans from the Deep South move north to industrial jobs.

1919–33   Prohibition. Chicago's transport links make it a natural place for alcohol manufacture and distribution. Armed crime mobs thrive.

1950s   In South Side clubs, rhythmic and electrified Chicago blues evolves.

1955   Richard J. Daley is elected mayor and dominates Chicago political life for 21 years.

1968   Police attack Anti-Vietnam War protesters in Grant Park during the Democratic National Convention.

1974   Completion of Sears Tower, the world's tallest building until 1996.

Late 1980s   DJs at Chicago's Warehouse nightclub create house music.

1992   A collapsing wall causes the Chicago River to flood the Loop.

1995   A heatwave kills 700 people.

2003   Runway at Meigs Field airport is bulldozed without warning by order of the mayor.

From the left: *Historic rail tickets; sign for Clarke House; the grave of Daniel Burnham; singing the blues*

GANGSTERS

Intended to encourage sobriety and family life, Prohibition (1919–33) provided a great stimulus to organized crime. The exploits of Chicago-based gangsters such as Al Capone became legendary. Though depicted frequently on films and TV, shoot-outs between rival gangs were rare. An exception was the 1929 Valentine's Day Massacre, when Capone's gang eliminated their archrivals in a hail of machine-gun fire. Wealthy enough to bribe corruptible politicians and police, the gangsters seemed invincible, but the gangster era—though not necessarily the gangs—ended with Capone's imprisonment in 1931 and the repeal of Prohibition.

Time to Shop

Below : *Keep on shopping*
Below right: *Inside
Woodfield Mall*

Chicago's shops can excite the purchasing passions of the entire Midwest while surprising and delighting visitors from much farther afield. The upscale malls and boutiques on and around

SPORTING SOUVENIRS

The city that produced basketball's Michael Jordan and made a celebrity of baseball's Sammy Sosa is unsurprisingly rich in sporting lore and offers much memorabilia and mementoes. Baseball's White Sox and Cubs both have outlets close to their stadiums, and that of the latter, the legendary Wrigley Field, has a souvenir-industry all of its own. The merchandise of Football's Chicago Bears and basketball's Chicago Bulls is also prevalent around the city.

the Magnificent Mile attest to the international nature of the city, while the plethora of smaller independent outlets show that the city has retained its own character against the onslaught of globalized retailing.

For designer clothing, the Miracle Mile is the showplace of Chicago. Men and women in pursuit of quality attire will find most major names represented in the high-rise malls along Michigan Avenue. For those who like a more personal shopping experience, a stroll around nearby Elm Street finds a clutch of elegant boutiques offering European haute couture and eager assistants. The same area hosts many of the city's major art galleries and antique dealers. More mid-range art and antique dealers are to be found in River West, while their brasher, funkier counterparts, are a feature in the shopping districts of Lake View and Wicker Park. Here there is also an abundance of outlets for extreme clothing, new and vintage, and bizarre household furnishings often made by local craftspeople.

Simple souvenirs can be found at the Magnificent Mile malls, but more choices at better prices are to be found among the touristy shops of Navy Pier. Alternatives to miniatures of high-rise

Below: Taking a break in Long Grove
Below left: Shopping on Michigan Avenue

buildings, such as Sears Tower and Hancock Tower, and T-shirts, plates and fridge magnets bearing images of the skyline seen from Lake Michigan include the genuine municipal cast-offs, such as sewer covers and parking meters, offered by the Chicago Store on E Pearson Street.

Sausages might seem an unlikely reminder of Chicago but the city has been shaped by people of Eastern European descent, with the result that Polish (and that of other Eastern Europeans nationalities) handmade sausages, with various meats, flavorings and spices, are a feature of many delis. For a quick bite, try the distinctive hot dogs (► 71) and deep pan pizza (► 67).

Surviving the rising tide of international chains, Chicago retains an impressive number of independent bookstores; 57th Street in Hyde Park holds several. Likewise, the city's strong jazz and blues pedigree is represented by specialist CD and vinyl outlets often featuring new Chicago-based musicians alongside established names.

THE LOOP

Historic department stores such as Carson Pirie Scott and Marshall Fields (► 72) are reminders of the glory days of The Loop, when it was the unchallenged social hub of the city. This role was ended by the retail and population shift to suburbia and the Loop became solely a place of work, symbolized by its high-rise office towers. Aided by a 1990s rejuvenation that saw 1920s-style lampposts and subway entrances appear, the Loop has enjoyed a minor revival. State Street is still the showpiece thoroughfare. Amid countless run-of-the-mill clothiers and shoe suppliers, State Street contains a plethora of long-established music stores and a surprising number of cigar retailers.

19

Out and About

BUS TOURS

Chicago Trolley Company
Tours in and around the Loop; hop on and off.
☎ 773/648-5000;
www.chicagotrolley.com

Tour Black Chicago
Tours revealing a century of African-American culture in Chicago.
☎ 773/684-9034; www.tourblackchicago.com

Chicago Hauntings
Tours of the city's haunted sites based on author Ursula Bielski's books on Chicago ghosts.
☎ 773/404-4346; www.chicagohauntings.com

Chicago Architecture Foundation
Architectural tours.
☎ 312/922-3432;
www.architecture.org

INFORMATION

SIX FLAGS GREAT AMERICA
Distance 43 miles (69km) from the Loop
✉ Gurnee, accessed from I-4 at 132 E Grand Avenue exit
☎ 847/249-4636;
www.sixflags.com
🎡 Late Apr–end Aug daily; Sep Sat, Sun
💲 Expensive (including all rides)

ORGANIZED SIGHTSEEING
To discover Chicago's rich yet diverse history and culture, take one or more of the tours offered by Chicago Neighborhood Tours (☎ 312/742-1190; www.chgocitytours.com). These include special interest tours focusing on topics such as WPA Murals, literary Chicago and public gardens. Chicago Architecture Foundation (☎ 312/ 922–TOUR; www.architecture.org) offers two-hour walking tours of the Loop's landmark buildings, as well as boat tours on the Chicago River. Spirit of Chicago (☎ 866/211–3804; www.spiritcitycruises.com) runs lunch, dinner or dinner-and-dance boat trips on Lake Michigan. The Noble Horse (☎ 312/266–7878; www. thenoblehorse. com) provides the chance to ride a horsedrawn buggy along the Magnificent Mile.

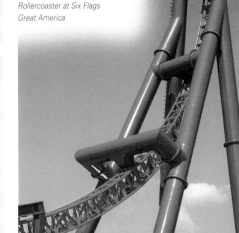

Rollercoaster at Six Flags Great America

EXCURSIONS

SIX FLAGS GREAT AMERICA

Gurnee, west of the city, is the home of Six Flags Great America, the Midwest's largest theme park, where in its five historically themed areas you will find exciting high-rise rollercoasters that reach speeds of 65mph (105kph), and other thrill rides—including a few for small children—plus spectacular shows, parades and special events. Be sure to sample the 996-seat Pictorium Theater, a breathtaking experience where films of action stunts, natural phenomena, and much more are projected with frightening realism onto a gigantic IMAX screen.

NORTH SHORE

The communities lining Lake Michigan north of Chicago are best toured as a whole by car, although many individual places of interest are easily reached by public transportation.

Evanston, Chicago's oldest and largest suburb, has upscale shops that lure many city-dwellers on weekend buying expeditions, and its two historic districts of 19th-century residences are pleasant. Evanston is also the site of Northwestern University, with its Block Museum of Art. The lakefront north of the university is ideal for strolling. Head for the 1873 Grosse Point Lighthouse and enjoy the lake view from its 113-ft (34-m) high tower. Continuing north, Wilmette holds the dome-topped Baha'i House of Worship, built over 40 years from 1920 and the first temple in the US for this religion. Farther north near Glencoe, in the 385-acre (156-ha) Chicago Botanic Gardens, you'll find well kept English rose, Japanese and Prairie gardens.

PULLMAN

Built in the 1880s for the 11,000 workers of the Pullman company, Pullman was protected as a National Historic Landmark in 1971, and many of its 1,800 original buildings remain. The creation of the town, although apparently an act of paternalism by company owner George M. Pullman, was inspired in part by a wish to keep his workforce away from the influence of Chicago's organized labor movement.

Walks

THE WEST LOOP

Begin at Sears Tower (1974), until 1996 the world's tallest building, with a fantastic view from its 103rd-floor Skydeck. Continue along Jackson Boulevard for the Chicago Board of Trade (1930), observing the trading from the visitors' gallery. Turn north along La Salle Street and peek inside the architecturally stunning Rookery (1880s). Continue north to the junction with Randolph Street to view the James R. Thompson Center (formerly known as the State of Illinois Center, and built in 1985), which has the Dubuffet sculpture, *Monument with Standing Beast,* looming outside. Inside, the 17-floor atrium echoes the building's curvilinear exterior and allows natural light to flood the interior. Cross Randolph Street to look inside the Richard J Daley Center (1965). Leave by the Washington Street side to view the 50-ft (15-m) tall untitled Picasso sculpture made from 162 tons of steel, across Washington Street from which is Joan Miró's sculpture *Chicago.*

Lunch and snacks Food stands lining the lower level of the James R. Thompson Center offer various fast food. The Berghoff Restaurant (➤ 70), a Chicago institution, serves hearty German fare. On the first floor of the Chicago Cultural Center is a café serving good coffee and snacks.

THE EAST LOOP

Stroll south along the increasingly tree-lined State Street, passing the glass and terra-cotta Reliance Building (1890s). Take a closer look at Miró's sculpture, *Chicago,* marking the plaza of 69 W Washington Street. Continue to Louis Sullivan's exquisite, early 20th-century Carson Pirie Scott & Co building, and cross to Dearborn Street for the Marquette Building (1895). Resume walking south to the Harold Washington Library Center. End the walk by strolling north along Michigan Avenue to the Chicago Cultural Center (1897), at the junction with Washington Street.

Wrigley Building

THE MAGNIFICENT MILE

Leave the Loop by walking north across the Chicago River on Michigan Avenue Bridge, which in 1920 facilitated the rise of the so-called Magnificent Mile as a fashionable retail and commercial area. Two of the first structures erected after the bridge was built were the Wrigley Building (1921–1924), to the left, and the Tribune Tower (1925), to the right. Farther north, opulent shops and hotels line Michigan Avenue. One of the liveliest stores is Nike Town, a retail showplace of the sports clothing manufacturer, between Erie and Huron streets. Cross to the west side of Michigan Avenue to see the excellent Terra Museum of American Art.

Lunch The Billy Goat Tavern (➤ 85) offers burgers and similar snacks. Pizzeria Uno (➤ 67, panel) is the place for deep-dish pizza. For more exotic fare, try Szechwan East (➤ 69), or for Italian food, Tucci Benucch (➤ 67).

THE MAGNIFICENT MILE: NORTH

Continue to the junction with Chicago Avenue and stop at the Historic Water Tower. Built in 1869 to house water-pumping equipment, the tower survived the fire and now holds a photographic gallery. A block north, on the junction with Chestnut Street, is the imposing Gothic form of the Fourth Presbyterian Church, used for lunchtime recitals. A short distance west, on Chestnut Street, there is more Gothic exuberance at the Quigley Seminary (1920s). Return to and cross Michigan Avenue to Water Tower Place, a glitzy, high-profile shopping mall. Across Delaware Place is the Palmolive Building, a 1930 art-deco landmark. Finish the walk at the John Hancock Center (1970), whose 94th-floor observatory affords stunning views across Chicago.

INFORMATION

Distance 1 mile (1.6km)
Time 2–3 hours
Start point ★ Michigan Avenue Bridge
⊞ H5/6
Ⓡ Red Line: Grand
🚌 3, 11, 29, 65, 147, 151, 157
End point John Hancock Center
⊞ H4
Ⓡ Red line: Chicago
🚌 145, 146, 147, 151
🍽 The Billy Goat Tavern (➤ 85); Pizzeria Uno (➤ 67, panel); Szechwan East (➤ 69); Tucci Benucch (➤ 67)

The Historic Water Tower

Chicago by Night

Above from left: the lit-up Buckingham Fountain; city's theater district; view of nighttime Chicago

CHICAGO BLUES

When the nationwide chain of House of Blues opened in the River West entertainment district in the 1990s, it marked a full circle for the city where South Side clubs gave birth to the urban electric blues. In such places, generally smaller and friendlier than the more tourist oriented North Side venues, it can still be heard.

LISTINGS

A free quarterly booklet, *Chicago Calendar of Events*, can be picked up at one of the visitors centers (► 90). Other sources for what's-on are the Friday *Chicago Tribune*, *Chicago* magazine and the weekly free newspapers *Reader* and *New City*.

SUN DOWN

After the sun sets, much of the Magnificent Mile and parts of the Loop are bathed in twinkling lights. The Wrigley Building seen from Michigan Avenue Bridge is famously stunning while the illuminated profile of the John Hancock Center makes the towering building seem even taller. From it, or the Loop's Sears Tower, a nighttime viewing reveals the grid-style patterns of the suburbs stretching into the distance and the blackness of Lake Michigan dotted by the lights of scattered ships.

WARM NIGHTS

Warm nights during spring, summer and autumn find Chicagoans enjoying the outdoors, making the most of bars and restaurants with patio tables. With its hotels and late-opening shops, the Magnificent Mile is lively after dark but there is more taking place in the nightlife strips of more residential neighborhoods. The Gold Coast sections of Division, Oak and Elm streets are worth a look, as are the main drags of Wicker Park and Lake View. More commercially oriented nightlife is found amid the themed bars and clubs of River West, although its broad streets are not well suited to casual strolling.

WINTER WONDERS

Cold and snowy Chicago may sometimes be, but dull it never is. The winter period marks a high-point of the cultural calendar with the classical concert, opera and ballet seasons fully into their stride, and a complete program of theater, rock and pop music.

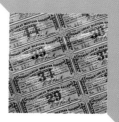

CHICAGO's
top 25 sights

The sights are shown on the maps on the inside front cover and inside back cover, numbered **1**–**25** from west to east across the city

Frank Lloyd Wright Home & Studio

DID YOU KNOW?

- 1867 Frank Lloyd Wright born in Wisconsin
- 1887 Arrives in Chicago
- 1909 Leaves Chicago to spend a year in Europe
- 1910 Opens Taliesin, a home and architectural school in Wisconsin
- 1936 Designs Fallingwater, a family home extending over a waterfall in a forest near Pittsburgh; a masterpiece of organic architecture
- 1938 Taliesin West, a winter home and school, opens in Arizona
- 1943 Finishes plans for New York's Guggenheim Museum; completed 16 years later
- 1959 Dies

INFORMATION

www.wrightpws.org

- Off map to west; Locator map A2
- 951 Chicago Avenue, Oak Park
- 708/848–1976
- Guided tours only: Mon–Fri 11, 1, 3; Sat–Sun 11–3.30
- Green line: Harlem
- Oak Park 23
- Few
- Moderate
- Ernest Hemingway Museum (➤ 55)

Frank Lloyd Wright's Drafting Room

An insight into the early ideas of one of the greatest and most influential architects of the 20th century. It is an essential stop for anyone interested in design, or in the ability of one man to realize his extraordinary vision.

Organic ideas Working for the Chicago architect Louis Sullivan, the 22-year-old Frank Lloyd Wright designed this home in 1889 for himself, his first wife and their children, and furnished it with his own pieces. The shingled exterior is not typical of Wright but the bold geometric shape stands out among the neighboring Queen Anne-style houses. Inside, the open plan, central fireplaces and low ceilings are the earliest examples of the elements that became fundamental in Wright's so-called Prairie School of Architecture. Particularly notable are the children's playroom, the high-backed chairs in the dining room and the willow tree that grows through the walls in keeping with Wright's theory of organic architecture—architecture in harmony with its natural surroundings.

Prairie views In 1893, Wright opened his own practice in an annex to the house: a concealed entrance leads into an office showcasing many of Wright's ideas, such as suspended lamps and an open-plan work space. The draftsmen once employed here on seminal Prairie School buildings worked in a stunningly designed room in sight of what was then open prairie.

Polish Museum of America

This museum enables many Chicago Poles to trace their roots, but it does not focus specifically on Chicago's Polish community. It is also home to cultural treasures threatened during the post-World War II years.

History East Europeans have long had a strong presence in Chicago, but no group among them has had greater visibility than Polish-Americans. Stanislow Batowski's immense painting, *Pulaski at Savannah*, dominates the museum's main room and sets off the collections remembering Pulaski and Kosciusko, two Polish soldiers who played significant roles in the American Revolution. The former was killed in battle and the latter helped lead the 1794 Polish uprising against Russia. Nearby are folk costumes, decorated Easter eggs, the costumes of the celebrated Shakespearean actress Helena Modrzejewska and remnants of the first Polish church in the United States.

Artistry Modestly occupying a corner is the immense stained-glass window that formed the centerpiece of the Polish culture exhibition at the 1939 New York World's Fair, its return home halted by the outbreak of war in Europe. The stairways and an upper floor are lined by Polish art, old and new. Amid many fine graphic works, look out for Mrozewski's cryptic 1936 depiction of H. G. Wells. A separate room holds mementos of Ignaczi Jan Paderewski, the pianist and composer whose US concert raised funds in the struggle for Polish independence in the early 1900s and who, in 1919, became the first prime minister of the Polish Republic. The last piano on which Paderewski performed is on display here, and so is the chair he used for all his performances.

DID YOU KNOW?

- 1851 Anton Smarzewski becomes Chicago's first Polish settler
- 1864 Peter Kiolbasa arrives in Chicago from Texas; entering public life, he becomes the city's first well-known Polish-American; he is nicknamed "honest Pete"
- 1869 Chicago's first Roman Catholic parish is established by Polish settlers
- 1871 German oppression of Poles causes a great rise in emigration to the US. Many settle in Chicago
- 1920 Poles become Chicago's largest foreign-born ethnic group
- 1937 Polish Museum opens

INFORMATION

www.pma.prcua.org
- E4; Locator map B2
- 773/384–3352
- Fri–Wed 11–4. Closed Thu
- Blue line: Division
- 9, 41, 56
- Few
- Donation
- Ukrainian Village (➤ 53)

Jane Addams Hull-House Museum

DID YOU KNOW?

- 1860 Jane Addams born in Cedarville, Illinois
- 1888 Visits England
- 1889 Opens Hull House with college friend Ellen Gates Starr
- 1909 Helps founding of National Association for Advancement of Colored People (NAACP)
- 1920 Helps founding of American Civil Liberties Union
- 1931 First American woman to receive Nobel Peace Prize
- 1935 Dies

INFORMATION

www.uic.edu/jaddams/hull/hull_house.html

F7; Locator map B3

800 S Halsted Street

312/413–5353

Tue–Fri 10–4, Sun noon–5

Blue line: UIC-Halsted

Halsted

8

Fair

Free

An impoverished immigrant's grim lot was made less miserable by the work of Jane Addams. In the late 19th century she created Hull House, a center in one of the city's neediest neighborhoods, and sparked many of the US's earliest social reforms.

A better life Inspired by a visit to London's East End, Jane Addams founded Hull House in 1889, offering English-language and US citizenship courses, child care, music and art classes and other services to the area's disparate ethnic groups—Germans, Irish, Poles, Ukrainians, Lithuanians and many more. She also campaigned, with much success, for improved sanitation, the end of child labor, a minimum wage, improved working conditions in factories and for numerous other causes. Serving some 9,000 people each week at its peak, Hull House grew into a complex of 13 buildings. The two buildings that remain sit elegantly, if incongruously, on the geometrically complex campus of the University of Illinois, most of which was designed by Walter Mesch of Skidmore, Owings & Merrill.

Prizewinning A 15-minute slide show tells the story of Addams and her settlement house, while the rooms of the main building are lined by furnishings and memorabilia including letters, photos, awards and books from the house library (which began with Addams's old college books). These items chart the course of Hull House's growth, its vital role in Chicago and the work that helped make Addams the most famous woman in America by the time she received the Nobel Peace Prize in 1931. The upper floor houses temporary exhibitions.

Graceland Cemetery

Founded in 1860, Graceland is Chicago's most prestigious cemetery and the last resting place of many of the city's most influential citizens with tombs to match their rank. Alongside great Chicagoans are a host of others, both famous and infamous.

Tombstone architecture Overlooked by lakeview apartments, its silence periodically broken by El trains, this is a distinguished place to be buried. Even here, noted city architect Louis Sullivan has left a mark with his elegant, ornate 1890 tomb for the steel magnate Henry Getty and his family. Sullivan is himself a Graceland resident, as are other Chicago architects Daniel Burnham, his partner, John Root, and modernist Ludwig Mies van der Rohe. Railway-carriage manufacturer George Pullman (► 21) is monumentalized by one of the largest tombs. Pullman died three years after the bitter 1894 strike. His grave was covered by tons of concrete to deter desecration.

Odd graves Among countless oddities to seek out (the free map issued from the office is essential) are the baseball adorning the resting place of National League co-founder William A. Hulbert and the unnerving statue, *Eternal Silence* by Laredo Taft, marking the tomb of hotel owner Dexter Graves.

DID YOU KNOW?

Also at Graceland:
- Philip D. Armour (meat-packing mogul)
- Marshall Field (department-store founder)
- Bob Fitzsimmons (boxer)
- Jack Johnson (boxer)
- John Kinzie (fur trapper, early settler)
- Victor Lawson (newspaper publisher)
- Potter Palmer (property tycoon)
- Bertha Palmer (wife of Potter, and society queen)

INFORMATION

- ✚ Off map to north; Locator map B2
- ✉ 4001 N Clark Street
- ☎ 312/525–1105
- 🕔 Office: Mon–Sat 8.30–4. Gates open during daylight hours
- Ⓠ Brown line: Irving Park. Red line: Sheridan
- 🚌 80
- ♿ Good
- 💳 Free
- ❓ Guided walking tours Aug–Sep by the Chicago Architecture Foundation (☎ 312/922–3432) and by Chicago Historical Society (☎ 312/642–6400)

Daniel Burnham's grave   29

Wrigley Field

The days of successive World Series wins may be a distant memory, but the baseball of the Chicago Cubs and the defiantly unmodern form of their stadium is as much a part of Chicago as the Water Tower and the El.

Landmark With its ivy-covered brick outfield wall, Wrigley Field provides the perfect setting for America's traditional pastime. Built in 1914, the stadium has steadily resisted Astroturf, and the game takes place on grass within an otherwise ordinary city neighborhood, now known as Wrigleyville. Denied car-parking space, most spectators have to endure densely packed El trains to reach the ballpark. Seating on the eastern side of Wrigley Field is single-tier and unroofed, exposing dedicated Cubs fans to the vagaries of Chicago weather, which during the April to October season can encompass anything from snow to sunshine and 100°F (38°C) temperatures.

Tradition Nearby residents watch the game from their windows, and some convert their roof space to box-like seating and charge admission. Others rent out their driveways for parking. Above the seats is the much-loved 1937 scoreboard on which the numbers are moved not by computer chips but by human hands. The floodlights did not appear until 1988, and then only after a fierce campaign of resistance. Someone in a high place may have objected: the first night game was abandoned because of rain.

Lincoln Park

This 1,200-acre (486-ha) green belt between the city and Lake Michigan has beaches, a zoo, a conservatory, a feast of statuary and much more. The park attracts Chicagoans of all kinds in both winter and summer.

Small beginnings Created out of sand dunes, swamp and the former city cemetery, Lincoln Park was established by the 1870s after its zoo (▶61) had been started with the gift of two swans from New York's Central Park. Evolving over a number of years through the contributions of various designers, it is now the oldest and most visited park in the United States. The gemlike 35-acre (14-ha) zoo houses lions, elephants, apes, polar bears and penguins in replicated habitats; close by, the Conservatory (1891) encompasses four separate greenhouses. Invitingly warm on cool and breezy Chicago days, the greenhouses provide balmy temperatures for dazzling tropical and subtropical blooms and seasonal displays.

Abraham Lincoln's statue in Lincoln Park

Beaches and bodies Tennis and badminton courts, putting greens and ponds navigable in rented paddleboats are dotted across the rest of the park, linked by walking, jogging and cycle tracks. Facing the lake are several small beaches, crowded on sunny weekends. At the south end of the park are the Chicago Historical Society (▶ 34) and the Couch Mausoleum, which holds a few of the 20,000 corpses once buried beneath the park's southernmost reaches.

HIGHLIGHTS

- Lincoln Park Zoo
- The Conservatory
- Bates Fountain (conservatory garden)
- The Standing Lincoln
- Couch Mausoleum
- Beaches

INFORMATION

- ✚ G/H1/2/3 and off map; Locator map B2
- ⊠ North of North Avenue, lining Lake Michigan
- ☎ Conservatory: 312/742–7736. Zoo: 312/742–2000
- ◷ Visit during daylight only
- 🍴 Cafeteria
- ♿ Good
- Ⓠ Red line: Armitage. Brown line: Fullerton (for zoo)
- 🚌 76, 77, 145, 146, 147, 151, 156
- 💵 Free (including zoo)
- ↔ Chicago Historical Society (▶ 34)

31

Sears Tower

DID YOU KNOW?

- Height: 1,454ft (443m)
- Height including antenna towers: 1,707ft (520m)
- Weight: 222,500 tons
- Square feet of floor space: 4.5 million
- Miles of plumbing: 25 (40km)
- Miles of electrical wiring: 20 (32km)
- Miles of telephone cable: 43 (69km)
- Elevator speed: up to 1,600ft (488m) per minute
- Number of windows: 16,100
- View from Skydeck in clear weather: 45–50 miles (72–80km)

INFORMATION

www.sears-tower.com
- ⊞ G7; Locator map D3
- ✉ 233 S Wacker Drive
- ☎ 312/875–9696
- ◔ Skydeck: May–end Sep daily 10–10; Oct–end Feb daily 9am–10pm; Apr 10–8. May be closed in high winds
- ⊪ Various restaurants and cafés
- ⊙ Brown and Orange lines: Quincy
- ⊟ 1, 60, 151, 156
- ⊛ Excellent
- ⊕ Moderate
- ⊡ The Rookery (➤ 33), Carson Pirie Scott & Co Store (➤ 35)

Although it is no longer the world's tallest building, the Sears Tower does rise higher than any other structure in this city. In addition to the unique and stylish architecture, it has the highest man-made vantage point in the western hemisphere.

Built from tubes From 1974 to 1996, the Sears Tower's 110 floors and 1,454-ft (443-m) height made it the tallest building in the world, rising from the Loop with a distinctive profile of black aluminum and bronze-tinted glass. Architect Bruce Graham, of Skidmore, Owings & Merrill, structured it around nine 75sq-ft (7sq-m) bundled tubes, which decline in number as the building reaches upwards. Aside from increasing the colossal structure's strength, this technique also echoes the stepback, New York skyscraper style of the late 1920s. Among the early tasks during the three-year construction was the creation of foundation supports capable of holding a 222,500-ton building. The two rooftop antennae were added in 1982, increasing the building's total height by 253ft (77m) and serving the many broadcasting organizations based inside the tower.

Seeing for miles Although the audiovisual presentation on Chicago at street level is uninspiring, the 103rd-floor Skydeck is not. Accessible via a 70-second elevator ride, it reveals a tremendous panorama of the city and its surroundings. In each direction, a recorded commentary describes the view and landmark buildings, seen here as few were ever intended to be seen: from above. Sears, the retail company that commissioned the building and used its lower floors, moved out in 1992. Note Alexander Calder's moving sculpture, *Universe*, in the lobby at the Wacker Drive entrance.

The Rookery

Designed by Daniel Burnham and John Wellborn Root in the 1880s, and later renovated by Frank Lloyd Wright, the Rookery is among Chicago's most admired landmarks.

Birdhouse After the Great Fire of 1871, birds took to roosting in the water-storage building that was temporarily City Hall. It was consequently nicknamed the Rookery. Public feeling dictated that the building that replaced it should formally take on this name. Rising 11 floors, the Rookery was among the tallest buildings in the world on completion and one of the most important early skyscrapers: the thick load-bearing brick and granite walls at the base, decorated with Roman, Moorish and Venetian (and several rook) motifs, support upper levels with an iron frame that enabled the structure to be raised higher than previously thought possible.

Interior treasures The façade, however, is scant preparation for the interior. The inner court is bathed in incredible levels of natural light entering through a vast domed skylight. Imposing lamps hang above the floor, and Root's intricate ironwork decorates the stairways that climb up to a 360-degree balcony. The white marble, introduced by Frank Lloyd Wright in 1905, increases the sense of space and brightness.

DID YOU KNOW?

- 1885 Burnham & Root commissioned by Central Safety Deposit Company
- 1886 Construction begins
- 1888 Construction completed
- 1905 Frank Lloyd Wright renovates lobby
- 1931 William Drummond undertakes further updating, including mechanical improvements
- 1970 Placed on National Register of Historic Places
- 1972 Designated Chicago City Landmark
- 1992 Renovation maintains Wright's ideas but restores original decoration

INFORMATION

- ⊞ G7; Locator map D3
- ✉ 209 S La Salle Street
- ☎ 312/553–6150
- ◐ Lobby open during business hours
- ⊙ Brown or Orange lines: Quincy
- ⊟ 1, 22, 60, 151
- ⅛ Good
- ⚑ Free
- ⇄ Sears Tower (► 32), Carson Pirie Scott & Co Store (► 35)

Top: spiral stairways
Left: the Rookery   33

Chicago Historical Society

INFORMATION

www.chicagohs.org
- G3; Locator map B2
- 1601 N Clark Street
- 312/642–4600
- Mon–Sat 9.30–4.30, Sun noon–5
- Big Shoulders Café
- Brown line: Sedgwick
- 11, 22, 36, 72, 151, 156
- Good
- Inexpensive; free Mon
- Lincoln Park (▶ 31), International Museum of Surgical Sciences (▶ 44)

Almost as old as the city itself, this institution not only has a fine collection of artifacts relating to the city's past, but also is a world leader in studying US history in general.

Chicago collections The society occupies a Georgian-style brick building constructed in 1932, with a modern, glass-walled extension. It is just inside Lincoln Park near the southwest entrance. Generations of Chicago schoolchildren have come here to learn about their city's history. From the Union Stockyards to the Chicago Bears, every major facet in Chicago's rise from swampland to metropolis is discussed and illustrated in the chronologically arranged galleries. A page from an 1833 *Daily News* debating the potential impact of the coming of railways, the city's first locomotive and a bright array of vintage rail company posters demonstrate the city's role as a transport center. A lively display describes the gangster era; elsewhere the Haymarket Riot and Pullman Strike are thoughtfully covered and placed in context as part of the growth of the city's blue-collar militancy. Other exhibits cogently outline the emergence of Chicago as a center of architectural innovation.

The American Wing Alongside temporary shows, the society's American Wing houses two exhibitions that explore US history via informative texts and an excellent collection of period items. "We The People" charts the nation's growth from the fight for, and acquisition of, independence to the creation of the constitution and Westward Expansion. "A House Divided" focuses on the North–South conflicts in the young nation, looking particularly at the issue of slavery and the events leading to the Civil War.

Carson Pirie Scott & Co Store

Probably no other store in the world has a more elaborately decorated exterior than that of Carson Pirie Scott & Co, created by the gifted and influential architect Louis Sullivan over a five-year period beginning in 1899.

Nature's art While Sullivan was a key figure in what became known as the Chicago School of Architecture, the group that after Chicago's Great Fire gave the city the earliest skyscrapers, it was for his finely realized ornamentation that he became best known. With the cast-iron embellishment of the Carson Pirie Scott & Co Store, Sullivan's predilection for flowing yet geometric forms reached new levels of artistry. Nowhere are his skills better expressed than in the store's corner entrance on State and Madison streets, and around the store's first- and second-floor windows, the showpiece windows intended to display merchandize.

Light and space The more austere terra-cotta-clad upper levels express the steel form of the building. The large windows span the entire width between the steel supports: known as "Chicago windows" and made possible by the invention of plate glass, they accentuate the horizontal, maximize the amount of natural light reaching the interior and strengthen the general sense of geometric cohesion. A 1979 renovation restored many of Sullivan's forgotten features.

DID YOU KNOW?

- 1856 Louis Sullivan born in Boston
- 1871–1874 Studies architecture at MIT and École de Beaux-Arts in Paris
- 1875 Moves to Chicago
- 1881 Forms architectural practice of Adler & Sullivan with Dankmar Adler
- 1886 Commences building of Chicago's acclaimed Auditorium Building
- 1890 Getty tomb completed for Graceland Cemetery
- 1924 *Autobiography of an Idea* is published, including Sullivan's phrase "form follows function." Sullivan dies impoverished

INFORMATION

- H6; Locator map E2
- 1 S State Street
- 312/641–7000
- Tue–Wed, Fri–Sat 9.45–5.45, Mon and Thu 9.45–7.30
- Blue line: Madison. Red line: Monroe
- 22, 23, 36, 56, 157
- Good Free
- Sears Tower (▶ 32), The Rookery (▶ 33), Chicago Cultural Center (▶ 38)

Wrigley Building

DID YOU KNOW?

- Architects: Graham, Anderson, Probst & White
- Excavation begins: Jan 1920
- Completion: South Building–April 1921; North Building–May 1924
- Height: 425ft (130m)
- Storeys: South–30; North–21
- Area: 453,433sq ft (42,124sq m)
- Office workers employed in building: 1,300
- Clock-face diameter: 19ft 7in (6m)
- Clock hour-hand length: 6ft 4in (1.9m)
- Clock minute-hand length: 9ft 2in (2.8m)

In a prime site on Michigan Avenue stands the 1920s Wrigley Building, an elegant monument to high-rise architecture and to the Chicago-based company that is still the world's major manufacturer of chewing gum.

Forever gleaming The Wrigley Building was partly modeled on the Giralda Tower in Seville, Spain, although the many ornamental features echo the French Renaissance. It is actually two structures rather than one. The North and South buildings stand behind a continuous façade linked by an arcaded walkway at street level and by two enclosed aerial walkways. The ornate glazed terra-cotta façade has never been restored, but has retained its original gleam. The effect is most pronounced at night, when banks of 1,000-watt bulbs illuminate the exterior.

INFORMATION

- ✚ H5; Locator map E2
- ✉ 400 N Michigan Avenue
- ☎ 312/923–8080
- 🕐 Usual business hours
- Ⓡ Red line: Grand
- 🚌 3, 11, 29, 65, 147, 151, 157
- ♿ Good
- 🖐 Free

Northern pioneer It is hard to believe today, but at the time of construction there were no office buildings north of the Loop. The Wrigley Building, raised at the same time as the Michigan Avenue Bridge, was always intended as the gateway to the city's so-called Near North neighborhoods. The building's offices were fully rented immediately after completion, and house public relations, advertising and publishing companies.

Terra Museum of American Art

With quality temporary and long-term exhibitions, the Terra Museum insightfully explores the development of art in the United States and the rise to international preeminence of some of the nation's artists.

Industrial art The Terra is a rarity among the nation's art museums in having been designed solely to display American art. The museum was created by wealthy industrialist-entrepreneur Daniel J. Terra—who built a fortune on fast-drying ink—to showcase his own collections. The museum also borrows works for the frequently outstanding temporary shows that highlight work by American artists who have been neglected or otherwise undervalued by mainstream art museums. Terra, who served as a cultural affairs ambassador in the Reagan administration, also opened a sister museum in Giverney, France, to display American works painted in that country. Inspired by New York's Guggenheim, the Terra's design includes ramps between floors so that you can start at the top level and wind your way down.

The galleries Following several Whistler etchings, the "Attitudes Towards Nature" gallery explores the changing face of the American landscape as depicted by its early painters, among them Thomas Cole (founder of the Hudson River School), Thomas Moran and Frederick Church. Subsequent rooms display works by important figures such as William Homer and George Caleb Bingham, and lead into walls of moderns including pieces by Joseph Stella, Edward Hopper and Milton Avery. A well-lit alcove is the setting for the "collection cameo," where a particular work is hung alongside a detailed accompanying text.

HIGHLIGHTS

- *The Jolly Flatboatman*, George Caleb Bingham
- *The Last of the Mohicans*, Thomas Cole
- *Our Banner in the Sky*, Frederick Church
- *The Checker Players*, Milton Avery
- *Brooklyn Bridge on the River*, Max Weber

INFORMATION

www.terramuseum.org
- H5; Locator map E1
- 666 N Michigan Avenue
- 312/664–3939
- Tue 10–8, Wed–Sat 10–6, Sun noon–5
- Red line: Grand
- 3, 11, 125, 145, 146, 147, 151
- Moderate donation; free Tue and first Sun of month
- Wrigley Building (➤ 36), Tribune Tower (➤ 39), Museum of Contemporary Art (➤ 54), IBM Building (➤ 57)
- Free guided tours: Tue–Fri noon and 2pm weekends

Top: The Last of the Mohicans *by Thomas Cole (1801–1848)*

37

Chicago Cultural Center

Even in a city so richly endowed with architectural marvels, the early 20th-century Chicago Cultural Center—nicknamed "the people's palace"—is a unique treasure housed in a most striking building.

The exhibitions The original building was designed and completed in 1897 by architects Holabird & Root, serving as the city's main public library until 1974. The Chicago Cultural Center mounts displays that usually focus on aspects of Chicago history and architecture. Several exhibits run concurrently. Much more impressive to first-time visitors is the sheer grandeur of the building, with its gleaming marble, stained glass and polished brass, all in beaux-arts style.

The architecture The Washington Street entrance leads visitors through hefty bronze doors set beneath a Romanesque portal into the main lobby, whose grand staircase is bordered by exquisite mosaics set into its white Carrara marble balustrades. A visitor information office occupies part of the next floor, as does the hall and rotunda of the Great Army of the Republic, another exhibition space, with Tennessee marble walls and mosaic tile floor, while the floor above holds the Preston Bradley Hall, whose awe-inspiring 38-ft (12-m) Tiffany-glass dome has been valued at $35 million. The main exhibition hall is on the top level, where gorgeously decorated columns rise to meet an immaculately coffered ceiling.

Tribune Tower

In the 1920s, the *Chicago Tribune* newspaper staged a competition for the design of its new premises. The contest attracted many leading architects, and the winning entry has become one of the most loved elements of this fashionable stretch of Michigan Avenue.

Modern medieval Although Eliel Saarinen's second-placed entry came to wield greater influence on the future of high-rise building, it was the neo-gothic design by John Mead Howells and Raymond Hood that took the $100,000 first prize. Using vertical lines of differing width and a buttressed tower, Howells and Hood created a 46-floor building that looks like an elongated medieval cathedral. The structure was completed in 1925.

Stone-studded The building is best admired from a distance, although the lobby displays two former *Tribune* front pages, one marking the Great Fire of 1871 and the other America's entry into World War I. You can watch WGN, the Tribune-owned radio station, through the street-level window of the studio. Embedded in the building's walls are stones from famous landmark buildings, pilfered by *Tribune* foreign correspondents at the request of Robert McCormick, the paper's larger-than-life publisher from 1910 until his death in 1955.

DID YOU KNOW?

Tribune Tower includes stones from:

● The Berlin Wall, Germany
● The Alamo, Texas
● The Great Wall, China
● Westminster Abbey, London
● Notre-Dame, Paris
● The Great Pyramid, Egypt
● St. Peter's, Rome
● The Colosseum, Rome
● Hans Christian Andersen's home, Denmark

INFORMATION

✛ H5; Locator map E1
✉ 435 N Michigan Avenue
☎ 312/222–3994
🕐 Normal business hours
Ⓜ Red line: Grand
🚌 3, 11, 29, 65, 147, 151, 157
♿ Good
💲 Free
↔ Wrigley Building (➤ 36), Terra Museum of American Art (➤ 37), Museum of Contemporary Art (➤ 54), IBM Building (➤ 57)

Top: a radio show in progress
Left: the Tribune Tower entrance

Art Institute of Chicago

INFORMATION

www.artic.edu

- ✚ H7; Locator map F3
- ✉ 111 S Michigan Avenue
- ☎ 312/443-3600
- 🕐 Mon, Wed–Fri 10.30–4.30, Tue 10.30–8, Sat 10–5, Sun noon–5
- 🍴 Café
- 🚇 Brown and Orange lines: Adams
- 🚌 3, 4, 60, 145, 147, 151
- ♿ Good
- 💵 Moderate; free on Tue
- ↔ Carson Pirie Scott & Co Store (▶ 35), Chicago Cultural Center (▶ 38), Grant Park (▶ 41)
- ❓ Free tours daily

Above: Grant Wood's American Gothic

40

Housed in a classically inspired building erected for the World's Columbian Exposition (1893), the Art Institute has an acclaimed collection of Impressionist paintings. But its galleries showcase much more, from arms and armor to the original trading room of the Stock Exchange.

Masterworks Except for the celebrated *American Gothic* by Grant Wood, which is displayed amid the American collections, the pick of the paintings is the European art grouped chronologically on the ground floor. No work receives greater notice and admiration than Seurat's expansive *A Sunday Afternoon on the Island of La Grande Jatte*, a pointillist masterpiece. Seminal works in adjacent galleries include haystacks by Monet, dancers by Degas, a self-portrait on cardboard by Van Gogh and the vibrant *Paris Street, Rainy Day* by Caillebotte. Among the many modern works are Picasso's *The Old Guitarist* and Hopper's moody *Nighthawks*.

Curiosities Everything from Chinese ceramics to Guatemalan textiles has a niche on the first floor. There is a huge collection of paperweights, and there are swords, daggers and chain mail. Leave time for the stunning 1898 Trading Room of the Chicago Stock Exchange, designed by Louis Sullivan and reconstructed here.

Grant Park

Planned by Daniel Burnham in 1909 as the centerpiece of a series of lake-front parks, Grant Park is a major festival venue that in its past has seen everything from an infamous violence-marred 1968 anti-Vietnam War demonstration to a papal Mass in 1979.

City views Far from being a bucolic extravaganza, Grant Park is essentially a succession of lawns criss-crossed by walkways and split in two by busy Lake Shore Drive. Bordered by the high-rises of the Loop and the expanses of Lake Michigan, Grant Park never lets you forget that you are in Chicago. Its Petrillo Music Shell provides a hospitable setting for summer concerts.

Evolving A section of today's park was designated as public land in 1836, but it reached its present size by expanding on to rubble from the 1871 fire, dumped as landfill in Lake Michigan. Among the features is the 1926 Buckingham Fountain, notable for its computer-choreographed display of colored lights dancing on the 1.5 million gallons (6.8 million liters) of water that are pumped daily. Taking shape on the park's northwestern edge, Millennium Park is a high-profile new public space, with an ice-rink and major additions that include Frank Gehry's 4,000-seat amphitheater and Anish Kapoor's reflective steel sculpture.

Events Grant Park is the venue for popular open-air events that attract millions of visitors every year, including blues, jazz and gospel music festivals, classical music concerts, and the Taste of Chicago when, for 11 days leading up to 4 July, more than 70 local restaurants set up tents to sell their gastronomical creations.

HIGHLIGHTS

- Blues Festival (June)
- Gospel Festival (June)
- Taste of Chicago (June–July)
- Independence Day concert and firework display (July)
- Jazz Festival (September)

INFORMATION

- H/J6/7/8/9; Locator map F3
- Bordered by N Michigan Avenue, E Randolph Drive, Roosevelt Drive and Lake Michigan
- Petrillo Music Shell concert information: 312/742–4763
- Visit during daylight hours only, except for special evening events
- Brown and Orange lines: Randolph, Madison or Adams
- 3, 4, 6, 38, 60, 145, 146, 147, 151, 157
- Good
- Free
- Carson Pirie Scott & Co Store (▶ 35), Chicago Cultural Center (▶ 38), Art Institute of Chicago (▶ 40), Field Museum of Natural History (▶ 42), John G. Shedd Aquarium (▶ 45), Adler Planetarium & Astronomy Museum (▶ 48)

Field Museum of Natural History

HIGHLIGHTS

- Sue
- "Traveling the Pacific"
- Stuffed gorilla
- Gem collection
- Pawnee earth lodge
- Tibet collections

INFORMATION

www.fmnh.org
- H/J8; Locator map F4
- E Roosevelt Road at Lake Shore Drive
- 312/922–9410
- Daily 9–5
- Coffee shop; McDonald's
- Orange line: Roosevelt
- Roosevelt Road
- 146
- Good
- Moderate; free Wed
- Grant Park (➤ 41), John G. Shedd Aquarium (➤ 45), Adler Planetarium (➤ 48)

An impressive exhibit in the dinosaur section

One of the world's great natural history museums, the Field displays superb exhibits drawn from all corners of the globe. After a strenuous round of viewing, ponder the fact that only around one percent of the museum's 20 million artifacts is on display.

The building The museum was completed in 1920, its cavernous galleries providing a home for a collection originally assembled for Chicago's 1893 World's Columbian Exposition. With its porticoes, columns and beaux-arts decoration, the imposing design sits rather uneasily with the needs of a modern museum, and sometimes the many rooms of exhibits from myriad eras and cultures can make for difficult viewing. Nonetheless, steady upgrading and innovative ideas in layout have made certain parts of the museum a rip-roaring success.

Great exhibits The outstanding sections include the dinosaur exhibits in which Sue, the most complete *Tyrannosaurus rex* ever found, takes pride of place; major ancient Egyptian artifacts, spanning 5000 BC to AD 300, arranged in and around the dimly lit and labyrinthine innards of a life-size, re-created tomb of a 5th-dynasty pharaoh; and "Traveling the Pacific," a powerful examination of cultural and spiritual life in Pacific cultures and the threats posed by the Western world's encroachment. Also noteworthy are the Native American displays and the sparkling gem collection, which includes pieces purchased in the 1890s from the famous Tiffany & Co jewellers.

Glessner House Museum

This home of a farm-machinery mogul, the only surviving example of the work of architect H. H. Richardson, profoundly influenced American domestic architecture and inspired designers such as Louis Sullivan. It is a beautiful house and still in beautiful shape.

Outside structure In 1885 a leading Chicago couple, John and Frances Glessner, commissioned Boston architect Henry Hobson Richardson to design a home for them. In contrast to the European revival-style homes dominating what was then Chicago's most fashionable neighborhood, the Glessners' house was given a fortress-like stone façade, and an L-shape that enabled its main rooms to face not the street, as was the vogue, but an inner courtyard. Initially, neighbors found the house objectionable, but many revised their opinions once invited in.

The Glessners' home In the house, oak beams and panels exude a warmth, and clever planning has created subtle distinctions between public areas and private ones. Richardson designed many furnishings, including the large oak desk in the library which, significantly for the time, was intended as a workplace for Mrs Glessner as well as for her husband. The Glessners' personal appreciation of art and design is reflected by their use of William Morris tiles and wall coverings, and the Isaac Scott ceramics and cabinets. John Glessner's photographs, which are on display in the house, confirm that the present-day appearance of the house and its furnishings is much the same as that enjoyed by the Glessners until their deaths in the 1930s. Rescued in 1966, Glessner House is now a National Historic Landmark.

DID YOU KNOW?

- 1838 Henry Hobson Richardson born in Louisiana
- 1859 Becomes the second American to study at the École de Beaux-Arts in Paris
- 1873 Establishes a reputation with the Romanesque-style church in Boston
- 1886 Dies just prior to the completion of the Glessner House

INFORMATION

www.glessnerhouse.org
➕ H9; Locator map C3
✉ 1800 S Prairie Avenue
☎ 312/326–1480
🕐 Guided tours: Wed–Sun 1, 2, 3
Ⓜ Red line: Cermak/Chinatown
🚌 1, 18, 38
♿ Few
💲 Moderate
↔ Clarke House (➤ 56)

43

International Museum of Surgical Sciences

HIGHLIGHTS

- *Professor W. T. Eckley's Dissecting Class* (photo)
- Drilled Peruvian skulls
- 15th to 16th-century amputation saw
- Needles and probes from Pompeii
- 1950s X-ray shoe-fitter
- Gallstone collection
- Civil War field amputation kit
- Reprint of Versalius's notebook
- Laennec's stethoscope

INFORMATION

www.imss.org

➕ H3; Locator map C2

✉ 1524 N Lake Shore Drive

☎ 312/642–6502

🕐 Tue–Sat 10–4 (also May–Sep Sun 10–4)

🚇 Brown line: Sedgwick

🚌 151

♿ Good 🅿 Moderate

🔁 Lincoln Park (➤ 31), Chicago Historical Society (➤ 34)

❓ Guided tour Sat 2pm

A drilled skull

When Peruvian surgeons drilled into patients' skulls 2,000 years ago, they probably never imagined that their work would be reviewed by doctors of the future as it is in the International Museum of Surgical Sciences, which traces medical advances and surgical skills through the ages.

House of health Founded in 1953, the museum is dedicated to enhancing the understanding of surgery past and present. Its several floors of exhibits, as well as innovative temporary shows, cover subjects related to health and medicine. The collection is housed in a stately mansion designed by Chicago architect Howard Van Doren Shaw and completed in 1917. A visit here will inform on surgical matters and provide an insight into the domestic arrangements of a wealthy family of early 20th-century Chicago.

Tools of the trade Among the oldest exhibits are drilled skulls discovered in ancient Peruvian temples, surgeons' tools found in excavations at the Roman town of Pompeii, and ancestor skulls used by shamans of Papua New Guinea to frighten evil spirits. Pioneering surgeons from various countries are commemorated with somber portraits and, in one case, a bronze replica of the surgeon's right hand. Many rooms are

packed with displays of fearsome needles, hooks and other sharp metalic things used for all manner of gouging, probing and extracting. Less unnerving are the early microscopes, the room filled with bulky X-ray machines and the stethoscope of one Doctor Theophile Laennec, which was designed to be fitted inside a top hat.

John G. Shedd Aquarium

Chicago's "Ocean-by-the-Lake" is the world's largest indoor aquarium, enhanced by a state-of-the-art oceanarium where dolphins and whales show off typical behaviours.

Aquarium A re-created Caribbean coral reef at the core of this imposing Greek-style building is home to barracuda, moray eels, nurse sharks and other creatures, who are fed several times daily by a team of microphone-equipped divers who describe the creatures, their habits and their habitat. Around the reef, denizens of the deep waters of the world occupy geographically arranged tanks. Look for the false-eye flashlight fish, born with the piscine equivalent of a flashlight; the mimic roundhead, able to deter predators by making its lower half resemble a moray eel; and the matamata turtle, so sluggish that you'll be lucky to see it move.

Oceanarium Dolphins and whales are the star attractions here. Five times daily, the dolphins display natural skills such as "spy-hopping," when a dolphin raises itself onto its tail to an audience seated around a re-created chunk of Pacific Northwest coast. Winding nature trails lead to the lower-level windows that provide an underwater view of the dolphins and whales. You also see a colony of penguins, and hands-on exhibits that describe facets of sea-mammal life, such as underwater movement, respiratory system, diet, mating habits and interaction with other sea creatures.

HIGHLIGHTS

- Pacific white-sided dolphins
- Beluga whales
- Sea otters
- Sea anemones
- Penguins
- Turtles

INFORMATION

www.sheddnet.org
- J8; Locator map F4
- 1200 S Lake Shore Drive
- 312/939–2438
- Daily 9–5 (Sat until 6), Memorial Day–Labor Day 9–6
- Soundings Restaurant; snacks from various stands at Bubble Net Food Court
- Orange line: Roosevelt
- Roosevelt Road
- 146
- Excellent
- Expensive. Aquarium free Thu; other exhibits reduced fee
- Grant Park (► 41), Field Museum of Natural History (► 42), Adler Planetarium (► 48)

Decorations on the aquarium door illustrate the sea life within

45

Navy Pier

Few visitor attractions anywhere in the world have a collection of stained-glass windows vying for attention with a Ferris wheel, but at Navy Pier they do just that, part of an expanding venue that mixes culture, cuisine, entertainment and retail.

History and cruises Opened in 1916, Navy Pier was part of architect Daniel Burnham's vision for a new Chicago and was intended to combine shipping with dining and entertainment. The former steadily disappeared and the pier declined until a 1990s makeover saw it re-emerge as a stylish family-aimed entertainment venue in the heart of the city. The pier has encouraged a revival of water activity with a plethora of pleasure cruises departing from its edge along Dock Street.

Culture and entertainment For thrills and spills, try Time Escape, a 3D ride catapulting visitors from the present day back to the Lake Michigan of 85 million BC and forward to Chicago in the 24th century. The daring can tackle Cliff Climb, a series of roped routes over a 180sq-ft (17-sq m) climbing surface, while the placid can test their putting skills across the miniature golf course. Other pursuits include the Chicago Children's Museum (▶ 61), the Chicago Shakespeare Theater (▶ 82) and the Smith Museum of Stained Glass, including a stained-glass portrait of basketball legend Michael Jordan.

A street performer on stilts at Navy Pier

Oriental Institute

The University of Chicago's Oriental Institute is a leader among museums and research centers specializing in the Middle East. The sheer volume of exhibits creates a powerful impression of ancient cultures.

The history In the 1890s, the newly founded University of Chicago was already showing off a modest collection of Middle East antiquities. As the university embarked on its own field trips the collections expanded significantly, and in 1919 the Oriental Institute was established. Since then, the institute's finds, and its acclaimed interpretation of them, have greatly enhanced the understanding and appreciation of the once mighty kingdoms of Egypt, Assyria, Anatolia, Mesopotamia and neighboring regions. The museum was purpose-built in 1931 by the firm of Mayers, Murray & Phillips, who included numerous Middle Eastern motifs. A major renovation during the 1990s restored many original architectural features.

The galleries Amid the mummy masks, royal seals and polished clay pots, several sizeable pieces stand out. Dominating the Egyptian section is an enormous statue of Tutankhamun, from his tomb in the Valley of Kings. In the Assyrian section is the human-headed winged bull, an immense sculpture that once stood in the palace of the powerful Sargon II (reigned 721–705 BC). Also from Sargon II's palace is a stone relief showing two officials. The museum's whole collection—so extensive that only a small fraction can be displayed at one time—spans about 3,000 years, from the 2nd millennium BC.

HIGHLIGHTS

- Tutankhamun statue
- Human-headed winged bull
- Relief from the tomb of Mentuemhat
- Striding lion
- Clay prism of Sennacherib
- Egyptian Book of the Dead
- Archaic-period bed
- Statue of Horus
- Mesopotamian four-faced god and goddess

INFORMATION

www.oi.uchicago.edu

Off map to south; Locator map C3

1155 E 58th Street

312/702–9520

Tue, Thu–Sat 10–4, Wed 10–8.30, Sun noon–4

Red line: Garfield

59th Street

4, 55

Good

Free

Du Sable Museum of African-American History (➤ 49), Museum of Science and Industry (➤ 50)

Top: Sumerian votive statues
Left: a sandstone statue of Tutankhamun

47

Adler Planetarium & Astronomy Museum

HIGHLIGHTS

- Sky Theater
- Apache Point Observing Station link-up
- Space Transporters
- Martian rocks
- Stranded in an Alien Lab

INFORMATION

www.adlerplanetarium.org

- J8; Locator map C3
- 1300 S Lake Shore Drive
- 312/322–STAR
- Mon–Fri 9.30–4.30, Sat–Sun 9–4.30 (1st Fri of month 9.30–10pm)
- Cafeteria
- Orange line: Roosevelt
- Roosevelt Road
- 146
- Good
- Inexpensive; free entry to building on Tue
- Grant Park (➤ 41), Field Museum of Natural History (➤ 42), John G. Shedd Aquarium (➤ 45)

Bringing close-up views of deep space to Chicagoans and other earthlings, the Friday evening Sky Show has helped the Adler Planetarium and Astronomy Museum to win local hearts since it opened in 1930.

Skywatching Max Adler, a Sears Roebuck executive, realized his ambition to put the wonders of the cosmos within the reach of ordinary people when he provided the money to have the western hemisphere's first modern planetarium built in Chicago. The planetarium holds one of the world's major astronomical collections. This landmark building is a dodecahedron in rainbow granite, decorated by signs of the zodiac and topped by a lead-covered copper dome. The fascinating Sky Show examines themes in astronomy using a multimedia theater and then the 68-ft (21-m) dome of the Sky Theater. Friday evenings the Sky Show displays live images from the observatory's computer-controlled telescope. The StarRider theater, presents digital, interactive comic voyages.

Finding space Among the permanent exhibits, Universe In Your Hands documents the early earth-centered view of the universe bolstered by

a selection of medieval telescopes, and Revolution in the Sky, shows how astrological discoveries revealed the greater importance of the Sun to our solar system. Other areas are devoted to how changing perceptions of the universe affected human culture, and the practicalities of exploring space with items from manned exploration and samples of moon and Martian rock.

Du Sable Museum

One of Chicago's unsung museums, this one chronicles aspects of black history, chiefly focusing on African-Americans but also encompassing African and Caribbean cultures.

Settlers The museum is named after Chicago's first permanent settler, Jean-Baptiste Point du Sable, a Haitian trader born of a French father and African slave mother. Further African-American arrivals came in three main waves—during the late 19th century and during the two World Wars—settling mostly on Chicago's South Side. Black businesses became established, while the expanding community provided the voter base for the first blacks to enter Chicago politics. Among the settlers were many musicians, and what became Chicago blues was born—an electrified urban form of rural blues fused with elements of jazz. The turbulent 1960s saw growing radicalism among Chicago's African-Americans, and the beginning of the rise to national prominence of South Side's Jesse Jackson.

Part of the display of African sculpture

Exhibits The first-floor rooms display items from the permanent collection, but there are also meticulously planned temporary exhibitions, while the Arts and Crafts Festival, displaying original works on African-American themes is held on the second weekend of July.

DID YOU KNOW?

- 1850 Passing of Illinois' Fugitive Slave Law makes Chicago an important stop on the "Underground Railroad" of escaped slaves
- 1871 First Chicago black elected to public office
- 1900 Chicago's black population: 31,150
- 1905 Founding of the nationally influential African-American-run newspaper, *Chicago Defender*
- 1919 What newspapers call a race riot leaves 38 dead
- 1940 Chicago's black population: 278,000
- 1950 Chicago's black population: 492,000
- 1968 Jesse Jackson founds PUSH on South Side
- 1983 Harold Washington is elected Chicago's first black mayor

INFORMATION

www.dusablemuseum.org
- Off map to south; Locator map C3
- 740 E 56th Place
- 773/947-0600
- Mon–Sat 10–5, Sun noon–5
- Red line: Garfield
- 59th Street 4
- Good
- Inexpensive; free on Sun

49

Museum of Science & Industry

INFORMATION

- Off map to south; Locator map C3
- 57th Street at Lake Shore Drive
- 312/684–1414
- Summer: daily 9.30–5.30; rest of the year: hours vary, call for times
- Several cafés
- Red line: Garfield
- 55th, 56th, 57th Street
- 6, 10
- Excellent
- Moderate; free on Thu; separate charge for Omnimax Theater
- Du Sable Museum of African-American History (➤ 49), Oriental Institute (➤ 47)

With 2,000 exhibits spread across 15 acres (6ha), this museum easily fills a day. Even know-it-all visitors find hours passing like minutes as they discover new things about the world—and beyond—at every turn.

Flying high The first eye-catching item is a Boeing 727 attached to an interior balcony. Packed with multimedia exhibits, the plane simulates a flight from San Francisco to Chicago, making full use of flaps, rudders and undercarriage, all fully explained. Other flight-related exhibits include a simulated mission aboard a naval F-14 fighter. Reflecting other modes of transport are the 500mph (804kph) Spirit of America car, a walk-through 1944 German U-boat and the Apollo 8 spacecraft. The moon-circling Apollo craft forms just a small part of the excellent Henry Crown Space Center, housed in an adjoining building.

Medical matters A 16-ft (5-m) high walk-through heart sits among exhibits detailing the workings of the human body. Close by, in the AIDS exhibit, imaginative devices explain much about viruses and the workings of the immune system. The display has a computer-generated voyage into the body, which illustrates the attack strategy of the HIV virus and the approaches used by scientists to combat it.

CHICAGO's
best

Neighborhoods

CHINATOWN

Other Chinese enclaves exist in Chicago, but the longest-established area—and what the city thinks of as Chinatown—is the eight blocks around the junction of Wentworth Avenue and Cermak Road, south of the heart of the city. Packed with restaurants and bakeries, herbalists and tea shops, Chinatown resounds to the snap of firecrackers each February during Chinese New Year, one of Chicago's liveliest festivals.

One of many busy restaurants in Chinatown

🚼 G9/10   🚇 Red line: Cermak/Chinatown   🚌 24

THE GOLD COAST

In the late 19th century, a top Chicago businessman astonished his peers by erecting a mansion home on undeveloped land well north of the Loop close to Lake Michigan. As others followed, the area became known as the Gold Coast, its streets lined by the elegant town houses of the city's well-to-do. Many of the homes remain, joined by ultra-luxurious apartment towers.

🚼 H3/4

HYDE PARK AND KENWOOD

Between Hyde Park Boulevard and the University of Chicago campus, Hyde Park became established, from the 1880s, as a leafy suburb complete with two parks designed by Frederick Law Olmsted and Calvert Vaux. Many early homes have been demolished, but some remain in Kenwood, north of Hyde Park Boulevard. Both areas are now populated predominantly by professionals, and have numerous bookstores and restaurants.

🚼 Off map to south   🚇 Red line: Garfield   🚂 Hyde Park-53rd   🚌 1, 4, 28, 51

THE LOOP

So-named for its position within the loop formed by the El, the Loop is Chicago's business district and the home of the city's most celebrated architecture. The Loop is the vibrant hub of the city by day—virtually deserted by night.

🚼 G/H6/7   🚇 All El lines converge on the Loop   🚌 Most north–south routes

MAGNIFICENT MILE

The favored shopping strip for wealthy Chicagoans, the section of Michigan Avenue between the Chicago River and Oak Street was named the Magnificent Mile by a property developer in the 1940s. The street's elegant stores, gleaming high-rise shopping malls and designer outlets pay some of the city's highest commercial rents.

➕ H4/5 🚇 Red line: Grand, Chicago 🚌 3, 11, 125, 145, 146, 147, 151

OAK PARK

From 1889, Frank Lloyd Wright added some 25 buildings in his evolving Prairie School style to the Victorian homes along the tree-lined streets of Oak Park, 8 miles (13km) west of the Loop. Ernest Hemingway (➤ 55) called it a town of "broad lawns and narrow minds."

➕ Off map to west 🚇 Metra Line West 🚉 Oak Park 🚌 23

PRINTER'S ROW

The industrial buildings lining Dearborn Street, which runs south from the Loop, were the core of Chicago's printing industry during the late 19th century. Many are now loft-style apartments, with galleries and restaurants.

➕ G7 🚇 Blue line: La Salle; Red line: Harrison 🚌 22, 62

RIVER NORTH

In the angle formed by the two branches of the Chicago River north of the Loop, this area of handsome warehouses is now filled with commercial art galleries, auction houses, eateries and nightspots.

➕ G/H5/6 🚇 Brown line: Chicago; Red line: Grand, Chicago 🚌 22, 37, 41, 65, 66

UKRAINIAN VILLAGE

Ukrainians settled this area off W Chicago Avenue during the early 1900s. Evidence of the old country includes St. Nicholas Cathedral (➤ 58), Ukrainian eateries and stores, a culture center and Ukrainian Independence Day festivities on 22 January.

➕ C5 🚇 Blue line: Chicago 🚌 66

A book market in full swing in Printer's Row

WICKER PARK AND BUCKTOWN

The 4-acre (1.5-ha) park on Damen Avenue that gives Wicker Park its name is enclosed by gray-stone mansions. These days Wicker Park and neighboring Bucktown (north of Milwaukee Avenue) are fashionably bohemian (if increasingly gentrified) and known for their alternative music clubs and coffee bars that regularly stage poetry readings and performance art events.

➕ C/D3/4

A Printer's Row mural illustrates the area's past

Museums

MICHIGAN AVENUE BRIDGEHOUSE MUSEUM

Housed in the southwestern tower of the Michigan Avenue Bridge, the Bridgehouse Museum documents the Chicago River and the vital part it played not only in facilitating the rise of the city of Chicago itself but in boosting the wealth of the entire nation. The northeast tower is due to became a cultural center.

✚ Michigan Avenue Bridge

BALZEKAS MUSEUM OF LITHUANIAN CULTURE

Regional folk costumes and other Lithuanian historical items form part of an extensive and absorbing collection.

✚ Off map to south ⊠ 6500 S Pulaski Road ☎ 773/582–6500 🚇 Daily 10–4 🚇 Orange line: Midway 🚌 53A 🚾 Few 🎟 Inexpensive

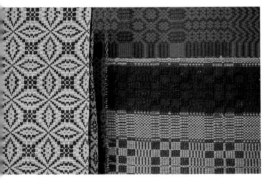

Display of textiles in the Balzekas Museum of Lithuanian Culture

MUSEUM OF CONTEMPORARY ART

Highlights from the permanent collection include the works of the Chicago-based Ed Paschke, and Richard Long's *Chicago Mud Circle* (1996), created directly on a gallery wall. The lower levels house temporary exhibitions and provide access to the Sculpture Garden.

✚ H5 ⊠ 220 E Chicago Avenue ☎ 312/280–2660 🚇 Tue 10–8, Wed–Sun 10–5 🚇 Red line: Chicago 🚌 157 🚾 Good 🎟 Moderate; free on Tue 5–8

MUSEUM OF CONTEMPORARY PHOTOGRAPHY

In addition to the museum's collection of American photography, you will find varied temporary exhibitions of contemporary photography from around the world.

✚ H7 ⊠ 600 S Michigan Avenue ☎ 312/344–7104 🚇 Mon–Fri 10–5, Sat noon–5 🚇 Red line: Harrison 🚌 1, 3, 4, 6, 38, 146 🚾 Good 🎟 Free

ERNEST HEMINGWAY MUSEUM

A collection remembering the Nobel Prize-winning writer who spent his first 18 years in Oak Park. Open the same hours and on the same street, at number 339 N, is Hemingway's birthplace.

➕ Off map to west ✉ 200 N Oak Park Avenue ☎ 708/848–2222 🕐 Mon–Fri, Sun 1–5, Sat 10–5 🚇 Green line: Harlem 🚉 Oak Park 🚌 23 ♿ Few 🎫 Moderate

DAVID AND ALFRED SMART MUSEUM OF ART

An eclectic collection, with works by Auguste Rodin, Albrecht Dürer and Mark Rothko, and furniture from Frank Lloyd Wright.

➕ Off map to south ✉ 5550 S Greenwood Avenue ☎ 312/702–0200 🕐 Tue–Fri 10–4 (Thu until 8), Sat–Sun 11–5 🚇 Red line: Garfield 🚉 59th Street 🚌 4 ♿ Good 🎫 Donations

SPERTUS MUSEUM OF JUDAICA

Torah scrolls, Hanukkah lamps and tools used in circumcision are among the decorative and religious objects spanning 5,000 years that form the core of this museum's extensive collection of Judaica. However, only a small selection can be shown at any one time. The richness of most exhibits contrasts strongly with the somber collection of Holocaust memorabilia.

➕ H7 ✉ 618 S Michigan Avenue ☎ 312/322–1747 🕐 Sun–Wed 10–5, Thu 10–7, Fri 10–3 🚇 Red line: Harrison 🚌 1, 3, 4, 6, 38, 146 ♿ Good 🎫 Inexpensive; free Fri

NATIONAL VIETNAM VETERAN'S ART MUSEUM

Paintings, sculpture, writing and photography from (mostly) American combatants in Vietnam fill this museum. Adding to the sense of despair evoked by many works are the guns and equipment, used by both sides, that share the gallery space. The effect can be harrowing; one reviewer called the collection "art in a state of shock."

➕ 1801 S Indiana Avenue

An exhibit from the Spertus Museum

Historic Buildings

MARQUETTE BUILDING

Completed in 1895, the Marquette Building is among the unsung masterpieces of Chicago architecture. It demonstrates the first use of the three-part "Chicago window"–plate glass spans the whole width between the building's steel supports. Lobby reliefs record the expedition of French Jesuit missionary Jacques Marquette; the entrance doors' panther heads are by Edward Kemeys, who is also responsible for the lions fronting the Art Institute of Chicago (➤ 40).
🔢 140 S Dearborn Street

CLARKE HOUSE (1830s)

The Clarke House (named after its original owner) is the oldest structure in Chicago. The interior has been restored to a mid-19th-century appearance.
🔢 H9 ☒ 1800 S Prairie Avenue ☎ 312/326–1480 ③ Guided tours: Wed–Sun noon, 1, 2. Guided tours including Glessner House: Fri noon; Sat–Sun noon, 1, 2, 3 🚇 Red line: Cermak/Chinatown 🚌 18th Street 🚌 1, 3, 4, 18 ♿ Few 💵 Moderate; can be combined with Glessner House

HISTORIC WATER TOWER (1869)

This pseudo-Gothic confection in yellow limestone, by William Boyington, is a city landmark.
🔢 H5 ☒ 800 N Michigan Avenue ☎ First-floor photography gallery 312/742-0808 ③ Mon–Sat 10–6.30, Sun 10–5 🚇 Red line: Chicago 🚌 11, 66, 145, 146, 147, 151 ♿ Few 💵 Free

RELIANCE BUILDING (1895)

Charles Atwood pre-empted the modern skyscraper with this building's steel skeleton and large bay

windows divided by slim terra-cotta mullions.
🔢 H6 ☒ 32 N State Street 🚇 Red or Blue lines: Washington 🚌 20, 22, 36, 56

ROBIE HOUSE (1910)

A famed example of Frank Lloyd Wright's Prairie School style of architecture. The horizontal emphasis reflects the Midwest's open spaces.
🔢 Off map to south ☒ 5757 S Woodlawn Avenue ☎ 708/848–1976 ③ Guided tours: Mon–Fri 11, 1, 3. Continuous tours: Sat–Sun 11–3.30 🚇 Green Line: Cottage Grove 🚌 59th Street 🚌 4 ♿ Few 💵 Free

The Historic Water Tower

Modern Buildings

IBM BUILDING (1971)
The 54 floors of Mies van der Rohe's last office building rise sleekly above the Chicago River. His bust is in the lobby.
✚ H6 **✉** 330 N Wabash Drive **Ⓡ** Red line: Grand **🚌** 29 **♿** Good

JAMES R. THOMPSON CENTER (1985)
This glass and steel edifice was designed by Helmut Jahn. Inside, a soaring atrium is lined with stores, restaurants and cafés; upper levels house state agencies.
✚ G6 **✉** 100 W Randolph Street **☎** 312/814–6684 **Ⓡ** Blue, Brown, Orange lines: Clark/Lake **🚌** 156 **♿** Good

James R. Thompson Center's massive atrium

JOHN HANCOCK CENTER (1970)
The tapering profile of the John Hancock Center, designed by Skidmore, Owings & Merrill, is a feature of Chicago's skyline; until 1974, when Sears Tower was completed, it was the world's tallest building. It has an observatory (➤ 60).
✚ H4 **✉** 875 N Michigan Avenue **☎** 312/751–3681 **Ⓢ** Skydeck Observatory: daily 9am–11pm **Ⓡ** Red line: Chicago **🚌** 145, 146, 147, 151 **♿** Good **Ⓤ** Skydeck Observatory: moderate

RICHARD J. DALEY CENTER (1965)
Jacques Brownson (of C.F. Murphy Associates) is credited with the center's design. Chiefly notable are the lobby's eternal flame memorial to the former mayor after whom the building is named, and the plaza's perplexing, untitled 1967 Picasso sculpture.
✚ G6 **✉** 50 W Washington Street **Ⓡ** Blue line: Washington **🚌** 6, 11, 20, 23, 56 **♿** Good

333 W WACKER DRIVE (1983)
The New York firm of Kohn Pedersen Fox struck a blow for postmodernism in Chicago with this acclaimed 36-floor building, slotted ingeniously into a triangular site next to the river.
✚ G6 **✉** 333 W Wacker Drive **Ⓡ** Blue, Brown, Orange lines: Clark/Lake **🚌** 16, 41, 125

MIES VAN DER ROHE IN CHICAGO

German-born Ludwig Mies van der Rohe, father of the International Style of architecture and one-time director of the German design school known as the Bauhaus, settled in Chicago in the 1940s, teaching at the Illinois Institute of Technology and redesigning it at the same time. Aside from the IBM Building and the institute, his most celebrated Chicago works are the glass and steel apartment buildings at 860–880 N Lake Shore Drive.

Places of Worship

Holy Name Cathedral

See Excursions for
BAHA'I HOUSE OF WORSHIP (▶ 21)

FOURTH PRESBYTERIAN CHURCH (1914)

This Gothic Revival church serves a congregation drawn from Chicago's moneyed élite. Occasional but enjoyable lunchtime concerts pack the pews.

🔲 H4 ✉ 126 E Chestnut Street
☎ 312/787–4570 🚇 Red line: Chicago
🚌 145, 146, 147, 151 ♿ Good

HOLY NAME CATHEDRAL (1878)

The atmospheric seat of the Catholic Archdiocese of Chicago. In 1926, gangster and former choirboy "Hymie" Weiss was machine-gunned to death on the steps.

🔲 H5 ✉ 735 N State Street
☎ 312/787–8040 🚇 Red line: Chicago
🚌 29, 36 ♿ Good

ST. NICHOLAS CATHEDRAL (1915)

A Byzantine-style cathedral, modeled on the Basilica of St. Sophia in Kiev, and serving Chicago Ukrainians. The cathedral adopted the Gregorian calendar only in 1969, and then amid great opposition.

🔲 C5 ✉ Junction of N Oakley Boulevard and W Rice Street ☎ 312/276–4537
🚇 Blue line: Chicago 🚌 66 ♿ Few

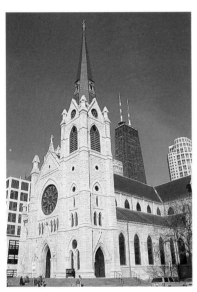

QUIGLEY SEMINARY AND ST. JAMES CHAPEL

An array of Gothic buildings, complete with leering gargoyles, lines a courtyard on Rush Street—west of the Magnificent Mile, between E Chestnut and E Pearson streets. Completed in the mid-1920s, the complex forms the Quigley Seminary and includes the St. James Chapel, decorated with stained-glass windows.

ST. STANISLAUS KOSTKA CHURCH (1881)

Raised to serve Chicago's Polish immigrants, this Renaissance-style church, modeled after a church in Krakow, Poland, quickly established the world's largest Catholic congregation.

🔲 B4 ✉ 1351 W Evergreen Avenue ☎ 773/278–2470 🚇 Blue line: Damen 🚌 52 ♿ Few

UNITY TEMPLE (1905)

Working to a tight budget, Frank Lloyd Wright used undecorated, reinforced concrete blocks —assembled into a series of interlocking sections— to create this temple for a Unitarian congregation in Oak Park. The furniture that Wright also designed for the building is still in use.

🔲 Off map to west ✉ 875 Lake Street, Oak Park
☎ 708/383–8873 🕐 Mon–Fri 10.30–4.30, Sat–Sun 1–4 🚇 Blue line: Harlem 🚌 Oak Park 🚌 23 ♿ Few

Parks, Gardens & Beaches

JACKSON PARK

In 1893, 27 million people attended the World's Columbian Exposition, held in what became Jackson Park, now a pleasant green space with sports courts, a Japanese garden and the Museum of Science and Industry (▶ 50).

➕ Off map to south ✉ Between S Stony Island Avenue and Lake Michigan 🚇 Red line: Garfield 🚉 55th, 56th, 57th Street 🚌 6, 10

NORTH AVENUE BEACH

The mile-long (2km) North Avenue Beach draws a cross-section of the city's population, and is ideal for lazy sunbathing. Volleyball nets are provided and there is a 1950s chess pavilion at the southern end of the beach.

➕ G/H1–3 ✉ Accessed from Lincoln Park 🚌 145, 146, 147, 151, 156

OAK PARK CONSERVATORY

Waterfalls, a herb garden and assorted desert and tropical vegetation are among the highlights of this undervisited place.

➕ Off map to west ✉ 615 Garfield Street, Oak Park 🚇 Blue line: Oak Park Avenue 🚉 Oak Park 🚌 23

OAK STREET BEACH

The closeness of the exclusive Gold Coast neighborhood helps make Oak Street Beach the gathering place for some of Chicago's richest and best-toned bodies.

➕ H4 ✉ Access from junction of N Michigan Avenue and E Lake Shore Drive 🚌 145, 146, 147, 151

WASHINGTON SQUARE

This was Chicago's first public park, and once buzzed with Sunday afternoon soap-box orators. Lunching office workers and shoppers are now its main users.

➕ G4 ✉ Bordered by W Walton Street and Delaware Place, and N Clark and N Dearborn streets 🚇 Red line: Chicago 🚌 22

GARFIELD PARK CONSERVATORY

Providing a refuge from urban Chicago, the conservatory has 5 acres (2ha) of tropical and subtropical plants, and is open daily 9–5 (Thu until 8), all year round. The highlights include extensive collections of palms, ferns and cacti. Chicagoans come here for expert gardening tips and for shows, when the opening hours are extended.

➕ 300 N Central Park Avenue

A sweeping view of the Chicago beaches

Views

BOAT TOURS

Almost any boat tour (➤ 20) brings fabulous views of the Loop's architecture, and the rest of the city strung along the Lake Michigan shoreline.

THE EL

As they loop the Loop from elevated rails, El trains on the Brown line bring spectacular close-up views of the district's high-rise architecture, its streets and its car parks, from unexpected angles.
➕ G/H6/7

The view from John Hancock Center's Skydeck Observatory

JOHN HANCOCK CENTER SKYDECK OBSERVATORY

Many Chicagoans prefer this 94th-floor outlook (over 1,000ft (305m) high, and close to other buildings and the lake) to the slightly higher but much busier Sears Tower Skydeck (➤ 32).
➕ H4 ✉ 875 N Michigan Avenue
☎ 888/875–VIEW ⏰ Daily
9am–11pm 🚇 Red line: Chicago
🚌 145, 146, 147, 151 ♿ Good
🍴 Moderate

SUNRISE AND THE LAKEFRONT TRAIL

Early birds can enjoy one of the best sunrises anywhere in the Midwest by joining the walkers, joggers and cyclists who start each morning on the 10-mile (16-km) Lakefront Trail through Lincoln Park (➤ 31). The spectacle created as the sun comes up over the lake, its rays reflected in the buildings of the Loop, makes the effort to be there well worth while.

LAKE SHORE DRIVE

By car, the best views of Chicago's high-rise skyline are from Lake Shore Drive, which cuts between the city and Lake Michigan. Passengers always relish the spectacle, although on weekdays drivers might well be too preoccupied with negotiating Chicago's traffic to enjoy the fine view.

MICHIGAN AVENUE BRIDGE

Night-time on this Chicago River crossing point reveals the Wrigley Building and Tribune Tower illuminated by floodlights; in the other direction loom the variously lit high-rises of the Loop.
➕ H5/6 ✉ Michigan Avenue between E Wacker Drive and E Illinois Street

PROMONTORY POINT

From this lakeside outlook some 5 miles (8km) south of the Loop, the Chicago skyline rises in great splendor. To the east, the curving Lake Michigan shoreline marks the northern edge of Indiana.
➕ Off map to south ✉ Eastern end of 55th Street

Attractions for Children

ARTIFACT CENTER AT THE SPERTUS MUSEUM
Interactive exhibits guide inquisitive minds through the mysteries of Middle Eastern archeology, and a re-created dig allows young hands to "discover" buried items from early Jewish civilizations, described in wall charts, maps and explanatory texts.
✚ H7 ☒ 618 S Michigan Avenue ☎ 312/322–1747 ④ Sun–Thu 1–430 ⓠ Red line: Harrison ▤ 1, 3, 4, 6, 38, 146 ⓖ Good ⓤ Inexpensive

CHICAGO ACADEMY OF SCIENCES— THE PEGGY NOTEBAERT NATURE MUSEUM
Lively exhibits explore the natural history of the Midwest, including a 28-ft (9-m) high greenhouse holding Butterfly Haven, and the inside story on the insect population of every household.
✚ G1 ☒ On the banks of North Pond in Lincoln Park (near Fullerton Parkway) ☎ 773/755–5100 ④ Mon–Fri 9–4.30, Sat–Sun 10–5 ⓠ Brown and Red lines: Fullerton ▤ 22, 36, 72, 156 ⓖ Good ⓤ Inexpensive; free Tue

CHICAGO CHILDREN'S MUSEUM
Spread across three floors are scores of lively and entertaining things to do for those aged under 12. These include workshop areas such as the Inventing Lab, where children can assemble flying machines, and Artabounds where they can create their own murals and sculptures. Programs change daily.
✚ J5 ☒ Navy Pier, 700 E Grand Avenue ☎ 312/527–1000 ④ Tue–Sun 10–5, Thu 10–4, 5–8 ⓠ Red line: Grand ▤ 29, 56, 65, 66 ⓖ Good ⓤ Moderate; free Thu 5–8

LINCOLN PARK ZOO
Lions, cheetahs, gorillas and chimpanzees are especially popular, along with the Children's Zoo, where tame and usually very furry animals can be stroked and cuddled.
✚ G2 ☒ Lincoln Park ☎ 312/742–2000 ④ Daily 9–6; Memorial Day–Labor Day 9–7 ⓠ Brown line: Armitage, Fullerton; Red line: Fullerton ▤ 151, 156 ⓖ Few ⓤ Free

RIVERWALK GATEWAY
Artist Ellen Lanyon tells the story of Chicago from 1673 to 2000 in 28 painted panels that stretch for 336ft (102m) along the walls of a passageway beneath Lake Shore Drive on the south bank of the Chicago River. The installation forms part of the Riverwalk and makes a free and fun way to learn something of the city's past.
✚ J6

Fun and games at the Chicago Children's Museum

Chicago's Best

What's Free

WATCHING THE MONEY-GO-ROUND

Speculating on pork belly futures is just one specialty of Chicago's financial dealers. At the Mercantile Exchange (⊠ 30 S Wacker Drive) visitors who love the sight of money changing hands but do not want to risk a cent watch from public galleries as millions of dollars are made and lost.

CHICAGO TRIBUNE FREEDOM CENTER

The printing works of the Chicago Tribune newspaper cost $187 million to build in 1982 and $100 million to renovate in 2001. See where the money went by taking a free 45-minute guided tour.
➕ F5 ⊠ 777 W Chicago Avenue ☎ 312/222–2116 🕐 Tours Tue–Fri 🚇 Blue line: Chicago 🚌 66 ♿ Good

HAROLD WASHINGTON LIBRARY CENTER

The US's largest public library is a state-of-the-art facility. Note its free exhibitions and eye-catching artworks. There is a children's library too, and free internet access.
➕ H7 ⊠ 400 S State Street ☎ 312/747–4300 🕐 Mon 9–7, Tue and Thu 11–7, Wed, Fri–Sat 9–4.30 🚇 Blue line: La Salle 🚌 11, 145, 146, 147 ♿ Good

Alexander Calder's Flamingo *at the Loop*

LOOP SCULPTURES (▶ 22)

Impressive sculptures stand on many plazas of the Loop. A short stroll will turn up contributions from Calder, Chagall, Miró and others. ⊠ Federal Center, Dearborn Street; Joan Miró ⊠ Washington Street; Marc Chagall ⊠ First National Plaza, Dearborn Street; Jean Dubuffet ⊠ James R. Thompson Center; Alexander Calder

MEXICAN FINE ARTS CENTER MUSEUM

Gain knowledge and appreciation of the diverse Mexican culture through this permanent collection of some 1,200 works by artists of Mexican nationality or descent. Exhibits include prints and drawings, photography, popular art, contemporary paintings and sculpture. This museum also mounts strong and varied temporary exhibitions, special events and arts education programs.
➕ D9 ⊠ 1852 W 19th Street ☎ 312/738–1503 🕐 Tue–Sun 10–5 🚇 Blue line: 18th Street 🚌 18 ♿ Good

CHICAGO's
where to...

Contemporary American

PRICES

Expect to pay per person for a meal, excluding drinks:

$ Up to $15
$$ $16–$30
$$$ $31–$50
$$$$ Above $50

All the restaurants listed are open daily for lunch and dinner unless otherwise stated.

At the luxury restaurants on these pages, the cost of dinner will easily exceed $70 excluding wine for two people, and lunch will typically cost around $50. Except in these luxury restaurants, dining in Chicago is often less expensive than in other major American cities. Expect to spend $6–$9 per person for breakfast, $8–$14 for lunch and $15–$25 for dinner excluding drinks and tip.

AMBRIA ($$$$)

A seasonally varied menu mates cuisines of France and the world with impeccable service and an immaculate setting.
✚ G2 ✉ 2300 N Lincoln Park West ☎ 773/472–5959 🕐 Dinner only. Closed Sun 🚇 Brown line: Sedgwick 🚌 156

CAFÉ ABSINTHE ($$$)

Dark, atmospheric and swanky, and excellent eclectic American cuisine with surprisingly little attitude.
✚ C3 ✉ 1954 W North Avenue ☎ 773/278–4488 🕐 Dinner only 🚇 Blue line: Damen 🚌 50, 56, 73

CHARLIE TROTTER'S ($$$–$$$$)

A fashionable dining place with superbly inventive, sometimes eccentric cooking.
✚ F2 ✉ 816 W Armitage Avenue ☎ 773/248–6228 🕐 Dinner only. Closed Sun, Mon 🚇 Brown line: Armitage 🚌 8, 73

CITÉ ($$$–$$$$)

A 70th-floor spot with rotating views taking in Lake Michigan and beyond. American French-influenced contemporary fare followed by a choice of cognacs and cigars.
✚ J5 ✉ N Lake Shore Drive, in Lake Point Tower ☎ 312/644–4050 🕐 Dinner only, brunch Sun 🚌 29, 56, 65, 66

FUSE ($$$)

The talk of fine-dining Chicago and the latest spot for chef Eric Aubriot to make an impression. Fuse blends a sleek design with the best inventive contemporary American fare.
✚ H6 ✉ Wacker Drive, Hotel 71 ☎ 312/346–7100 🚇 Red line: Lake, Blue line: Clark/Lake 🚌 8, 73

MK ($$–$$$)

Understated chic in a former paint factory, which chef Michael Kornick has turned into a venue for trendsetting concoctions, including lobster in many guises.
✚ G5 ✉ 868 N Franklin Street ☎ 312/482–9179 🚇 Brown line: Chicago 🚌 66

ONE SIXTYBLUE ($$$)

Striking décor and cutting-edge cuisine in this River West eatery. French-influenced fare includes delicate use of sauces and spices.
✚ E6 ✉ 160 N Loomis Street ☎ 312/850–0303 🕐 Dinner only. Closed Sun 🚇 Green line: Ashland 🚌 9

TRIO ($$$$)

Chef Shawn McLain provides startling presentations and flavors. One of the most coveted reservations in town.
✚ Off map to north ✉ 1625 Hinman Avenue, Evanston ☎ 847/733–8746 🕐 Dinner only Sat–Thu. Closed Sun 🚇 Purple line: Davis Street

312 CHICAGO ($$)

Winning fusion of contemporary American ideas and Italian cuisine.
✚ G6 ✉ 1136 N La Salle Street ☎ 312/696–2420 🚇 Brown or Orange lines: Washington, Green line: Clark/Lake 🚌 156, 157

Steaks, Ribs & Chops

CHICAGO CHOP HOUSE ($$–$$$)

The ribs, steaks and chops here are large and juicy enough to satisfy even the most demanding red-meat eaters. All meals begin with a fresh green salad and a loaf of wholewheat bread.

✚ G5 ✉ 60 W Ontario Street ☎ 312/787–7100 🕐 Dinner only weekends 🚇 Red line: Grand 🚌 125

ELI'S THE PLACE FOR STEAK ($$–$$$)

Noted for perfectly cooked T-bone steaks. The liver-and-onion appetizer is worth tasting, and don't miss the cheesecake.

✚ H5 ✉ 215 E Chicago Avenue ☎ 312/642–1393 🕐 Dinner only weekends 🚇 Red line: Chicago 🚌 3, 66

GENE & GEORGETTI ($$$)

Many feel that this steakhouse—complete with the men's-club décor, gruff waiters and deliciously thick cuts of meat—is the best in the city. Non-carnivores beware though, there's scant choice to satisfy you.

✚ G5 ✉ 500 N Franklin Street ☎ 312/527–3718 🚇 Brown, Purple lines: Merchandise Mart 🚌 37

LAWRY'S THE PRIME RIB ($$–$$$)

The primest of prime rib—the only option on the dinner menu here—is accompanied by such traditional favorites as Yorkshire pudding, mashed potatoes and salad or an enormous baked potato.

✚ H5 ✉ 100 E Ontario Street ☎ 312/787–5000 🕐 Dinner only weekends 🚇 Red line: Grand 🚌 125

MAGNUM'S PRIME STEAKHOUSE ($$–$$$)

In contrast to many longer established Chicago steakhouses, Magnum's has a modern feel and is ideally located in the River North entertainment area. The steaks are top notch and for the less hungry eaters, chicken, ribs and seafood are offered as well.

✚ G5 ✉ 225 W Ontario Street ☎ 312/337–8080 🕐 Dinner only 🚇 Brown line: Chicago or Merchandise Mart 🚌 65, 125

MORTON'S OF CHICAGO ($$–$$$)

Chicago takes steak seriously, and this is one of the best places to eat it. Porterhouses grilled to perfection are the stock-in-trade.

✚ H4 ✉ 1050 N State Street ☎ 312/266–4820 🕐 Dinner only 🚇 Red line: Chicago 🚌 36

RUTH'S CHRIS STEAKHOUSE ($$–$$$)

The Chicago branch of the big US steakhouse chain opened in 1992 and quickly made its mark. It serves substantial steaks, lamb, veal and pork, all topped with sizzling butter.

✚ G6 ✉ 431 N Dearborn Street ☎ 312/321–2725 🕐 Dinner only Sat. Closed Sun 🚇 Blue, Red lines: Jackson 🚌 22, 36

ALL-NIGHTERS

Do you get the munchies at 4am? You won't go hungry in Chicago. In addition to Tempo (► 71), 24-hour options include Hollywood Grill (✉ 1601 W North Avenue ☎ 773/ 395–1818); Clarke's (✉ 2441 N Lincoln Avenue ☎ 773/472–3505); and Lazo Tacos (✉ 2009 N Western Avenue ☎ 773/486–3303), for inexpensive Mexican fare.

French

MEXICAN FARE

There's no need to run for the border for Mexican fare and margaritas. Chicago's array of fresh Mex includes Su Casa (🖂 49 E Ontario Street ☎ 312/943–4041); Barro Cantina (🖂 163 W North Avenue ☎ 312/266–2484); and Lincoln Park's Twisted Lizard (🖂 1964 N Sheffield Avenue ☎ 773/929–1414).

ALBERT'S CAFÉ AND PATISSERIE ($–$$)

Open daily for breakfast, lunch and dinner in the Gold Coast, Albert's offers simple but delicious French-influenced fare and a tempting selection of pastries and cakes.
➕ G4 🖂 52 W Elm Street
☎ 312/751–0666
🚇 Red line: Division
🚌 22, 29, 36, 70

BISTRO CAMPAGNE ($$$)

Intimate setting for quality French cuisine from a small but well-chosen menu; come early in the week to avoid a crown scene.
➕ Off map to northwest
🖂 4518 N Lincoln Avenue
☎ 773/271–6100 🍴 Dinner only; Sun brunch 🚇 Brown line: Western 🚌 11, 49, 78

EVEREST ($$$$)

This 40th-floor restaurant commanding spectacular views—beloved of financial wheeler-dealers—offers an updated and sometimes inspiring look at chef Jean Joho's native Alsace. The Loop location, prices and standards of cooking are all breathtakingly high.
➕ G7 🖂 440 S La Salle Street
☎ 312/663–8920 🍴 Dinner only. Closed Sun, Mon 🚇 Blue line: La Salle 🚌 22

LA PETITE FOLIE ($$$)

Classical French fare in a minimalist setting in a Hyde Park shopping mall. The chef hits a home run with the escargot and smooth crème brulee.
➕ Off map to south
🖂 1504 E 55th Street
☎ 773/493–1394 🍴 Lunch Tue–Fri; dinner Tue–Sun 🚇 Red line: Garfield 🚌 55th, 56th, 57th 🚌 6, 10

LE FRANÇAIS ($$$$)

Since the 1970s, the impeccable fare and extraordinary wine list have been drawing diners to this classic culinary destination about an hour outside the city.
➕ Off map 🖂 269 S Milwaukee Avenue, Wheeling
☎ 847/541–7470 🍴 Dinner only Sat–Mon. Closed Sun
❓ Best reached by car

MON AMI GABI ($$–$$$)

A replica turn-of-the-century Parisian bar in the Lincoln Park neighborhood, and an affable setting for the downing of oysters or main dishes that include the house specialty of steak fries.
➕ G2 🖂 2300 N Lincoln Park West (in the Belden-Stratford hotel) ☎ 773/348–8886
🍴 Dinner only 🚌 151, 156

THE DINING ROOM ($$$$)

Spread across two sumptuously furnished floors, this restaurant in the luxurious Ritz-Carlton Hotel offers matchless contemporary French cuisine from the *carte* or as a fixed-price meal.
➕ H5 🖂 Ritz-Carlton Hotel, 160 E Pearson Street
☎ 312/226–1000 🍴 Dinner only 🚇 Red line: Chicago
🚌 125, 157

Italian

AL'S ITALIAN BEEF ($)
The menu may be limited but for an Italian beef sandwich, Al's has been unmatched since 1938. Several locations.
➕ G5 ✉ 169 W Ontario Street ☎ 312/943–3222 🚇 Brown and Purple lines: Merchandise Mart 🚌 65

CLUB LUCKY ($–$$)
The Italian menu is long at this trendy venue in Backtown, though the food tends to take second place to the socializing.
➕ H4 ✉ 1824 W Wabansia Street ☎ 773/227–2308 🚇 Blue line: Damon 🚌 7

COCO PAZZO ($$–$$$)
Delectable, mostly Tuscan cuisine in a comfortable setting enhanced by exposed ceiling beams. Tremendous daily specials and desserts; you can watch as your food is being prepared in the kitchen.
➕ G5 ✉ 300 W Hubbard Street ☎ 312/836–0900 🕐 Dinner only weekends 🚇 Red line: Grand 🚌 11, 156

LA STRADA ($$)
Well-presented, mostly northern Italian fare, served beneath crystal chandeliers in a very elegant setting.
➕ H6 ✉ 155 N Michigan Avenue ☎ 312/565–2200 🚇 Brown, Orange lines: Randolph 🚌 38, 56, 156

MIA FRANCESCA ($$)
There is always a wait at this favorite of Chicago natives. Excellent seafood specials and wonderful red-sauced fare, but it's the pasta in large amounts and top-notch pizza that make this undersized eatery one of Lake View's most popular.
➕ Off map to north ✉ 3311 N Clark Street ☎ 773/281–3310 🕐 Dinner only 🚇 Brown, Red, Purple lines: Belmont 🚌 22, 77

SCOOZI! ($$)
A vivacious spot for inventive Italian fare, Scoozi! is huge and often crowded with a young group. Look out for the giant tomato over the door.
➕ G5 ✉ 410 W Huron Street ☎ 312/943–5900 🕐 Dinner only Sun 🚇 Brown line: Chicago 🚌 37, 41

SPIAGGIA ($$$)
Steamed mussels in garlic and tomato broth is just one of the specialties of this celebrity favorite. The adjoining Spiaggia Café is less costly and less formal, and serves excellent pizza and pasta dishes.
➕ H4 ✉ 980 N Michigan Avenue ☎ 312/280–2750 🕐 Dinner only Sun 🚇 Red line: Chicago 🚌 145, 146, 151

TUCCI BENUCCH ($–$$)
For Miracle Mile shoppers who cannot bear to leave the area, this is located in a major mall (▶ 73) and offers straightforward Italian fare in a faux Italian country-house setting.
➕ H4 ✉ 900 N Michigan Avenue ☎ 312/226–2500 🚇 Red line: Chicago 🚌 145, 146, 147, 151

CHICAGO PIZZA

The first deep-dish pizza was created in 1943 at Chicago's Pizzeria Uno. The thick but light crust and a generous smothering of tomato sauce and mozzarella cheese, combined with a variety of toppings, helped make the Chicago pizza a full meal in itself, unlike the thin-crusted New York version. Pizzeria Uno is deservedly as popular as ever.
➕ H5 ✉ 29 E Ohio Street ☎ 312/321–1000 🚇 Red line: Grand 🚌 36

The finest traditional deep-dish pizza is on the menu also at Gino's East (✉ 633 N Wells Street ☎ 312/943–1124 🚇 Red line: Chicago 🚌 3, 11, 125, 145, 146, 147, 151) and Lou Malnati's Pizzeria (➕ G5 ✉ 439 N Wells Street ☎ 312/828–9800 🚇 Brown line: Merchandise Mart 🚌 37, 65, 156).

Asian

DIM SUM

Served by many Chinese restaurants at lunchtime, dim sum is the term for small dishes wheeled around on trolleys. Stop a server who has dishes that look appetizing and take your pick. Popular dishes include *cha sil bow*–steamed pork bun; *gai bow*–steamed chicken bun; *chern goon*–spring rolls; and *sil mi*–steamed pork and shrimp dumpling. When you've eaten your fill, you will be charged by the plate.

ARUN'S ($$$$)

Superb Thai fare, with subtle spicing reflecting the exceptional talent in the kitchen.
➕ Off map to north ✉ 4156 N Kedzie Avenue
☎ 773/539–1909 🕐 Dinner only. Closed Mon 🚇 Brown line: Kedzie 🚌 80, 82

BEN PAO ($$)

Inventive and inspired take on Chinese regional dishes, served under subdued lighting. Dim sum on weekends.
➕ G5 ✉ 52 W Illinois Street
☎ 312/222–1888 🚇 Red line: Grand 🚌 36

EMPEROR'S CHOICE ($$–$$$)

At this small, intimate restaurant portraits of former Chinese emperors hang above diners feasting on some of Chinatown's most creative seafood dishes. For a special occasion order Peking duck a day in advance.
➕ G10 ✉ 2238 S Wentworth Avenue ☎ 312/225–8800
🚇 Red line: Cermak/Chinatown 🚌 24

GARLIC & CHILI HEALTHY THAI CUISINE ($)

Great value hole-in-the-wall Thai spot in the Gold Coast, offering creative twists on classic Thai dishes and many vegetarian options.
➕ G4 ✉ 1232 N La Salle Street ☎ 312/255–1717
🚇 Red line: Clark/Division 🚌 11, 156

INDIA HOUSE ($–$$)

Spacious and comfortable River North setting for extensive choice of Indian standards, including an array of tandoori dishes and numerous vegetarian dishes.
➕ G5 ✉ 159 W Grand Avenue
☎ 312/645–9500 🚇 Red line: Grand 🚌 22, 65

JOY'S NOODLE AND RICE ($)

Great value Thai dishes served without fuss; portions are modest so order plenty. The patio is lovely on sunny days.
➕ Off map to north ✉ 3257 N Broadway ☎ 773/327–8330
🚇 Brown, Red lines: Belmont 🚌 36

KLAY OVEN ($$$)

One of Chicago's most acclaimed Indian restaurants. Traditional dishes are expertly prepared and stylishly presented by attentive, friendly staff in a sumptuous setting.
➕ G5 ✉ 414 N Orleans Street
☎ 312/527–3999 🕐 Dinner only weekends. Closed Mon
🚇 Brown line: Merchandise Mart 🚌 37, 41

LE COLONIAL ($$$)

This French-Vietnamese hot spot started in New York, then expanded to LA, San Francisco and Chicago. Rattan furniture and palm trees set the mood, as does an exotic drink in the sultry upstairs bar.
➕ H4 ✉ 937 N Rush Street
☎ 312/255–0088 🚇 Red line: Chicago 🚌 145, 146, 147, 151

PASTEUR ($$$)

Red snapper and steamed bass are among

the specialties at this inviting, romantic Vietnamese restaurant in Edgewater. Named after the Saigon street where the owners had their family home.

🚻 Off map to north ✉ 5525 N Broadway ☎ 773/878–1061 🚇 Red line: Granville 🚌 136

PENNY'S NOODLE SHOP ($)

This Thai-inspired noodle shop draws raves for both traditional dishes and creative interpretations. Also at Diversey Parkway.

🚻 Off map to north ✉ 3400 Sheffield Avenue ☎ 773/281–8222 🚇 Brown, Red, Purple lines: Belmont 🚌 7

RA SUSHI ($–$$)

Loud music and eye-grabbing décor fails to detract from the quality of the food, which includes a range of sushi and tempura dishes, and much more. Near the Magnificent Mile.

🚻 H4 ✉ 1139 N State Street ☎ 312/274–0011 🚇 Red line: Clark/Division 🚌 22, 36

STANDARD INDIA ($)

The utilitarian décor is not promising, but the Indian food is good. There is a menu, but many diners opt for the pricewise buffet.

🚻 Off map to north ✉ 917 W Belmont Avenue ☎ 773/929–1123 🕐 Closed Tue 🚇 Brown, Red lines: Belmont 🚌 77

STAR OF SIAM ($$)

Hustle and bustle describe this no-frills River North Thai outpost, which serves

excellent classics like Pad Thai and chicken satay. The large windows and airy atmosphere are a plus.

🚻 H5 ✉ 11 E Illinois Street ☎ 312/670–0100 🚇 Red line: Grand 🚌 29, 36

SZECHWAN EAST ($$–$$$)

Chic and stylish option for zesty Szechwan food. The weekday lunch buffet is good value.

🚻 H5 ✉ 340 E Ohio Street ☎ 312/255–9200 🚇 Red line: Grand 🚌 3, 66, 157

THAI CLASSIC ($–$$)

The inexpensive lunch specials and wonderful Sunday buffet are worth sampling, but the regular menu is no less impressive. Bring your own bottle.

🚻 Off map to north ✉ 3332 N Clark Street ☎ 773/404–2000 🚇 Red line: Addison 🚌 22

THAI PASTRY & RESTAURANT ($)

Regulars are drawn by the subtle curry dishes, while the pad thai is equally noteworthy; good value lunch specials on weekdays.

🚻 Off map to north ✉ 4925 N Broadway ☎ 773/784–5399 🚇 Red line: Argyle 🚌 36

VONG'S THAI KITCHEN ($–$$)

Innovative mixing of Thai flavorings and spices with eclectic international fare; sample the "Black Plate" of appetizers for the idea.

🚻 G5 ✉ 6 W Hubbard Street ☎ 312/644–8644 🕐 Dinner only Sat–Sun 🚇 Red line: Grand 🚌 29

IF YOU'RE VEGETARIAN

Most Chinese, Thai and Vietnamese restaurants offer meat-free versions of their staples, as do Indian eateries; Italian restaurants (► 67) are another likely possibility. Even amid the chop houses and barbecued rib joints, there's usually some selection. Among the almost exclusively vegetarian restaurants try Chicago Diner (✉ 3411 N Halsted Street ☎ 773/935–6696) and Dharma Garden Thai (✉ 3109 W Irving Park Road ☎ 773/588–9140).

German & East European

THE TASTE OF CHICAGO

Chicagoans love to eat and do so with gusto by the thousand at the Taste of Chicago festival, one of the city's most eagerly awaited events, which is held annually in Grant Park. For the 11 days before 4 July around 100 local restaurants dispense their creations at affordable prices from open-front stalls. Free musical entertainment keeps toes tapping.

BARBAKAN RESAURANT ($)

Unprepossessing décor, complete with ageing formica tables, conceals delicious Polish food at appealingly low prices; the soup options change daily. In the strongly Polish neighborhood of Jackowo.
+ Off map to north
⊠ 3145 N Central Avenue
☎ 773/202–8181 Ⓜ Blue line: Belmont ▯ 85

BERGHOFF RESTAURANT ($–$$)

German staples such as *sauerbraten* and *bratwurst* are served in a cavernous, oak-paneled dining room, along with home-brewed German-style beer. Well-prepared American dishes are also on the menu. An institution founded in 1893.
+ H7 ⊠ 17 W Adams Street ☎ 312/427–3170
Ⓒ Closed Sun Ⓜ Blue, Red lines: Jackson ▯ 1, 7, 60, 126, 151

CAFÉ LURA ($)

Live music and cabaret provides reason to call here in the evenings, but worth a stop earlier in the day for the full-bodied Polish fare.
+ Off map to north ⊠ 3185 N Milwaukee Avenue
☎ 773/737–3033 Ⓜ Blue line: Belmont ▯ 56, 77

GLUNZ BAVARIA HAUS ($$)

Schnitzel, roast pork and duck feature on the long menu of German–Austrian cuisine in this Lincoln Park/De Paul eatery, which also offers potent German beers.
+ Off map to north
⊠ 4128 N Lincoln Avenue
☎ 773/472–4287 Ⓒ Closed Mon Ⓜ Brown line: Irving Park
▯ 11, 80

HEALTHY FOOD LITHUANIAN RESTAURANT ($)

Beneath the Lithuanian scenes that decorate the walls, this spartan South Side spot serves dishes from the Baltic country, including mushroom barley soup and homemade sausages.
+ F11 ⊠ 3226 S Halsted Street ☎ 312/326–3724
Ⓜ Orange line: Halsted ▯ 8

RUSSIAN TEA TIME ($$)

Caviar, roast pheasant, iced vodka and other Russian gastronomic specialties.
+ H7 ⊠ 77 E Adams Street ☎ 312/360–0000 Ⓒ Lunch only Mon Ⓜ Brown, Orange lines: Adams ▯ 1, 7, 60, 126, 151

SAK'S UKRAINIAN VILLAGE RESTAURANT ($)

A lively favorite for traditional Ukrainian stuffed cabbage, chicken Kiev, soups and *blintzes*.
+ C5 ⊠ 2301 W Chicago Avenue ☎ 773/278–4445
Ⓒ Closed Mon Ⓜ Blue line: Damen ▯ 66

SZALAS ($)

Designed as a mountain chalet with food and features from Poland's Podhale region; near Midway airport.
+ Off map to south ⊠ 5214 S Archer Avenue ☎ 773/582–0300 Ⓒ Dinner only
Ⓜ Orange line: Pulaski ▯ 62

Quick Bites

ANN SATHER'S ($)
A venerable coffee shop where Swedish fare such as cranberry pancakes tops the list of favorites.
🚹 Off map to north ✉ 929 W Belmont Avenue ☎ 773/348–2378 🕐 Breakfast, lunch, dinner 🚇 Brown, Red lines: Belmont 🚌 77

BIG BOWL CAFÉ ($–$$)
Delectable Asian noodle dishes, and much more, served in very big bowls.
🚹 G5 ✉ 6 E Cedar Street ☎ 312/640–8888 🕐 Dinner only Sun 🚇 Brown line: Chicago 🚌 37, 41

BOX CAR CAFÉ ($)
Offers a range of regular diner dishes but the main talking point at is this Lincoln Park/De Paul stop is the delivery of desserts and drinks by model train.
🚹 E1 ✉ 723 W Wrightwood Avenue ☎ 773/325–9560 🚇 Brown, Red lines: Fullerton 🚌 11

ED DEBEVIC'S SHORT ORDER DELUXE ($–$$)
Great burgers, sandwiches and milkshakes served to the background sound of 1950s and 1960s music.
🚹 G5 ✉ 640 N Wells Street ☎ 312/664–1707 🕐 Breakfast, lunch, dinner 🚇 Brown line: Chicago 🚌 37, 41

LEO'S LUNCHROOM ($)
Breakfast all day, salads and sandwiches for lunch, and ultra-affordable dinner specials that change nightly.
🚹 D3 ✉ 1809 W Division Street ☎ 773/776–6509 🕐 Closed Mon 🚇 Blue line: Division 🚌 70

LOU MITCHELL'S ($)
A friendly, modestly sized diner, founded in the 1930s and still serving great omelettes.
🚹 F7 ✉ 565 W Jackson Boulevard ☎ 312/939–3111 🕐 Lunch only. Closed Sun 🚇 Blue line: Clinton 🚌 7, 126

MAY STREET CAFÉ ($)
Fast and tasty dishes drawn from popular dishes of Latin America and the Caribbean; west of Chinatown.
🚹 E10 ✉ 1146 W Cermak Street ☎ 312/421–4442 🕐 Lunch only Sun 🚇 Red line: Cermak 🚌 21

STELLA'S DINER ($–$$)
When a craving for traditional diner fare strikes, Stella's burgers and milkshakes fit the bill.
🚹 Off map to north ✉ 3042 N Broadway ☎ 773/472–9040 🚇 Brown line: Wellington; Red line: Belmont 🚌 36

TEMPO ($)
Coffee shop with fluffy omelettes served in skillets, sandwiches, steaks and stir-fry dishes in an otherwise pricey neighborhood.
🚹 H4 ✉ 6 E Chestnut Street ☎ 312/943–4373 🕐 Open 24 hours 🚇 Red line: Chicago 🚌 36

TWIN ANCHORS ($–$$)
Simply the best place for ribs, which was once an Al Capone hangout.
🚹 G3 ✉ 1655 N Sedgwick Street ☎ 312/266–1616 🕐 Dinner only Mon–Fri 🚇 Red line: Clybourn; Brown line: Sedgwick 🚌 37

CHICAGO HOT DOGS

To a Chicagoan, a hot dog is not merely a frank in a bun. The true Chicago hot dog is a Viennese beef sausage smeared with ketchup, mustard, relish, onions and hot peppers to taste. Brightly lit hot-dog outlets are a feature of the city, and each has its devotees. Among them are Gold Coast Dogs
🚹 H6 ✉ 159 N Wabash Avenue, and other locations throughout the city ☎ 312/917–1677 🕐 Breakfast, lunch, dinner. Closed Sat–Sun 🚇 Red line: Grand 🚌 29, 36

Malls & Department Stores

CHINATOWN SHOPPING

For shoppers who venture from the better-known retail areas into Chinatown (▶ 52), rewards are plentiful in the form of entertaining emporia squeezed between the countless restaurants that line Wentworth Avenue, immediately south of Cermak Road. Check out World Treasures or Chinatown Bazaar for a wide assortment of Asian delights, and Woks 'n' Things selling kitchen utensils and general gifts. Within a few strides, you can also pick up a bag of fortune cookies at Fortella and choose from a vast selection of teas at Ten Ren Tea.

THE ATRIUM MALL

Diverse stores provide an excellent excuse to stroll around the spectacular second floor of this dazzling atrium, a pastiche of glass, marble and steel, with an impressive waterfall.

➕ H6 ✉ James R. Thompson Center, 100 W Randolph Street ☎ 312/346–0777 🚇 Blue, Brown, Orange lines: Clark/Lake 🚌 156

CARSON PIRIE SCOTT & CO STORE

Though better known for its exterior architecture (▶ 35), the store has provided middle-class Chicagoans with good clothing, cosmetics and household accessories for years.

➕ H6 ✉ 1 S State Street ☎ 312/641–7000 🚇 Blue line: Madison; Red line: Monroe 🚌 22, 23, 36, 56, 157

CHICAGO PLACE

A seven-floor branch of Saks Fifth Avenue department store is an anchor tenant among the classy retailers in this towering construction. Drop into Chiaroscuro to admire artworks and ornaments, explore the Slavic gifts and art in Russian Creations, or snap up an affordable city souvenir in Love From Chicago. There is a food hall on the top floor.

➕ H4 ✉ 700 N Michigan Avenue ☎ 312/266–7710 🚇 Red line: Chicago 🚌 145, 146, 147, 151

THE JEWELER'S CENTER

Jewelry and related products are sold in more than 140 outlets on 13 floors; if you can't find what you're looking for here, you never will.

➕ H6 ✉ 5 S Wabash Avenue ☎ 312/853–2057 🚇 Brown, Orange lines: Madison 🚌 38

MARSHALL FIELD'S

Chicagoans adore this department store, which carries clothing, household goods, jewelry, exotic foods, books and more. There are several branches in Chicago, but this is the best. The building has a Tiffany-glass dome, and the interior design outdoes Carson Pirie Scott and adds glamor. The store's own Frango Mints, sold in the basement Market Place section, make a good Chicagoland souvenir.

➕ H6 ✉ 111 N State Street ☎ 312/781–1000 🚇 Blue, Red lines: Washington 🚌 6, 11, 29, 36, 44, 62, 146

NAVY PIER

Some 60 shops are gathered in this complex of restaurants and entertainments. If you're ready to buy souvenirs as gifts, this is not a bad place to trawl.

➕ J5 ✉ 700 E Grand Avenue ☎ 312/595–PIER 🚇 Red line: Grand 🚌 29, 56, 65, 66

NEIMAN-MARCUS

Exclusive, elegant clothing is the forte of handsome Neiman-Marcus, which also sells beauty products and fancy food stuffs. Looking around is good fun, even if you can't afford to buy.

➕ H5 ✉ 737 N Michigan

Avenue ☎ 312/642–5900
🚇 Red line: Chicago 🚌 145, 146, 147, 151

900 NORTH MICHIGAN

This gleaming marble high-rise consumes an entire city block. Restaurants, cinemas and stores are grouped around a six-floor atrium; a branch of New York's Bloomingdale's is an anchor. There are also many smaller, exclusive stores, including Gucci and Gallery Lara, where exquisite glass sculptures sell for tens of thousands of dollars.
🗺 H4 ✉ 900 N Michigan Avenue ☎ 312/915–3916
🚇 Red line: Chicago 🚌 145, 146, 147, 151

SEARS

With few frills, Sears simply delivers what people need, be it clothing, household appliances, tools or jewelry, at a price they can afford.
🗺 G6 ✉ 2 N State Street
☎ 312/373–6000 🚇 Brown, Green or Red lines: State
🚌 Any Loop

SHOPS AT NORTH BRIDGE

Another Magnificent Mile mall, this one includes branches of AIX Armani, Body Shop and Spa Nordstrom, and several children's stores including Lego, which also offers the Construction Zone play area.
🗺 H5 ✉ 520 N Michigan Avenue ☎ 312/327–3200
🚇 Red line: Chicago 🚌 145, 146, 147, 151

SHOPS AT THE MART

Most of the vast Merchandise Mart is closed to the public, except for the first two floors, which woo shoppers with clothing stores, gift shops and the ubiquitous food court. For more than 50 years, the Kennedy dynasty owned this River North behemoth.
🗺 G5 ✉ 350 N Wells Street
🚇 Brown, Purple lines: Merchandise Mart 🚌 37

WATER TOWER PLACE

Packing these seven floors are clothing stores for men, women and children that span Abercrombie & Fitch, North Beach Leather, Baby Gap and Victoria's Secret. There are also jewelers, art galleries, home-furnishing emporiums such as Brookstone and Calypso 968, and perfumeries. In addition, there are cinemas and restaurants, and specialty retailers such as Accent Chicago and the Water Tower Clock Shop. You can rest next to the indoor shrubbery and waterfalls, or be decadent and treat yourself to some Godiva chocolates.
🗺 H4 ✉ 835 N Michigan Avenue ☎ 312/440–3165
🚇 Red line: Chicago 🚌 145, 146, 147, 151

THE MAKING OF THE MAGNIFICENT MILE

No Chicago shopper could be unaware that most top-class stores are gathered along the section of Michigan Avenue known as the Magnificent Mile (► 53). Many stores appeared here following the 1920s opening of the river bridge linking Michigan Avenue to the Loop, but the "Magnificent Mile" concept was a 1940s idea that eventually mutated into today's rows of marble-clad towers, mostly built during the 1970s and 1980s.

Clothes

CURIOUS CLOTHING

Should the sensible buying of sensible clothes for sensible everyday wear suddenly become a stultifyingly dull pursuit, you can let your sartorial imaginations run riot at Chicago Costume Company (✉ 1120 W Fullerton Parkway). This enormous store carries hundreds of outrageous costumes, masks and assorted outlandish accessories, for sale or rent, for the dresser who dares.

AGNES B
When money is no object look to this chic French designer to help you look like a sophisticated Parisian woman. Just off Michigan Avenue.
✚ H5 ✉ 46 E Walton Street
☎ 312/642–7483 Ⓠ Red line: Chicago 🚍 145, 146, 147, 151

BANANA REPUBLIC
The hugely popular local branch of the nationally known supplier of quality casualwear.
✚ H5 ✉ 744 N Michigan Avenue ☎ 312/642–0020
Ⓠ Red line: Chicago 🚍 145, 146, 147, 151

BARNEYS NEW YORK
The Chicago branch of a Manhattan store noted for chic women's clothing and its fine menswear.
✚ H4 ✉ 25 E Oak Street
☎ 312/587–1700 Ⓠ Red line: Chicago 🚍 145, 146, 147, 151

BROOKS BROTHERS
Well-made attire for men, in conservative styles, plus some equally straightforward clothing for women.
✚ H5 ✉ 713 N Michigan Avenue ☎ 312/915–0060
Ⓠ Red line: Chicago 🚍 145, 146, 147, 151

CHANEL BOUTIQUE
Breathe in the expensive perfumes, browse the top-of-the-line women's clothing and eye the gorgeous baubles in the jewelry section; it's all in a day's shopping for the seriously wealthy.
✚ H4 ✉ 935 N Michigan Drive (in the Drake Hotel)
☎ 312/787–5500 Ⓠ Red line: Chicago 🚍 145, 146, 147, 151

HOT THREADS
Clubwear, beachwear and lots of generally daring glamorwear for women, plus shoes, boots and accessories.
✚ Off map to north ✉ 3223 N Clark Street ☎ 773/665–9988 Ⓠ Brown and Red lines: Belmont 🚍 22, 36

J CREW
Classic modern clothes, shoes, and accessories for young men and women at work and play.
✚ H4 ✉ 900 N Michigan Avenue ☎ 312/751–2739
Ⓠ Red line: Chicago 🚍 145, 146, 147, 151

LORD & TAYLOR
Lovely, classic clothes, shoes and accessories for men and women in Water Tower Place.
✚ H4 ✉ Water Tower Place, 835 N Michigan Avenue
☎ 312/787–7400 Ⓠ Red line: Chicago 🚍 145, 146, 147, 151

PETITE SOPHISTICATE
An impressive assortment of stylish business and leisure clothing for smaller-than-average women.
✚ H4 ✉ 430 N Michigan Avenue ☎ 312/494–9218
Ⓠ Red line: Chicago 🚍 145, 146, 147, 151

PRADA
Three levels of clothing and accessories from the Italian designer.
✚ H4 ✉ 30 E Oak Street
☎ 312/951–1113 Ⓠ Red line: Chicago 🚍 145, 146, 147, 151

Accessories & Vintage Clothes

THE ALLEY

If your idea of an accessory is a Zippo lighter or a Che Guevara belt buckle, the Alley Stores, a group of alternative clothing stockists, is just the place to find it; also leather jackets and motorcycle boots.

🏠 Off map to north ✉ 3228 N Clark Street ☎ 773/883–1800 🚇 Brown or Red lines: Belmont 🚌 22, 36

BEATNIX

Packed from floor to ceiling, this stash of wild and unbelievable attire is Disneyland for the daring dresser.

🏠 Off map to north ✉ 3400 N Halsted Avenue ☎ 773/281–6933 🚇 Brown, Red lines: Belmont 🚌 152

BELMONT ARMY

What began as a army surplus store has expanded over three floors to become a top Chicago spot for hiking boots, backpacks and lots more for the outdoor life.

🏠 Off map to north ✉ 945 W Belmont Avenue ☎ 773/549–1038 🚇 Brown or Red lines: Belmont 🚌 77

THE DAISY SHOP

Gloves, handkerchiefs and jewelry feature among the used designer accessories; there are shelves of flowing chiffon dresses.

🏠 H4 ✉ 67 E Oak Street ☎ 312/943–8880 🚇 Red line: Chicago 🚌 145, 146, 147, 151

HERMÈS OF PARIS

Chicago branch of the Parisian fashion house, and a certainty for lovely scarves, handbags, ties and leather items.

🏠 H4 ✉ 110 E Oak Street ☎ 312/787–8175 🚇 Red line: Chicago 🚌 145, 146, 147, 151

RAGSTOCK

The quantity of used clothing is huge, and prices are very low. It takes time to sort through the dross, but you can find some great bargains. Upstairs from Hollywood Mirror.

🏠 H6 ✉ 226 S Wabash Avenue ☎ 312/692–1778 🚇 Blue line: Madison 🚌 22, 23, 36, 56, 157

TIFFANY & CO

The famous New York jeweler offers a stunning assortment of stones, plus superb watches, crystal, china and more.

🏠 H4 ✉ 730 N Michigan Avenue ☎ 312/944–7500 🚇 Red line: Chicago 🚌 145, 146, 147, 151

URBAN OUTFITTERS

Up-to-the-minute gear to match the hippest accessories and funky items for the home.

🏠 H4 ✉ 935 E Walton Street ☎ 312/640–1919 🚇 Red line: Chicago 🚌 145, 146, 147, 151

WACKY CATS

Vintage attire for men and women and particularly strong on bridal and formal dresses and lingerie; also stocks reproduction flapper dresses complete with feather boas.

🏠 Off map to north ✉ 3012 N Lincoln Avenue ☎ 773/929–6701 🚇 Brown line: Paulina 🚌 9, 11, 77

BUTTON UP!

At Tender Buttons (✉ 946 N Rush Street) the thousands of styles on sale are displayed with a museum-like reverence, and are complemented by a fine selection of Edwardian cuff links.

Art, Antiques & Collectibles

COLD CLIMATE COLLECTIBLES

Chicago's severe winters may be one reason why the arts of the Inuit peoples of Alaska, Siberia and Canada seem to have particular appeal for the city's art collectors. Such items are the stock-in-trade of two outlets: The Alaska Shop (⊠ 104 E Oak Street) and The Orca Art Gallery (⊠ 812 N Franklin Avenue), which besides offering items for sale has regular exhibitions.

BROADWAY ANTIQUES MARKET

The 85 dealers at this two-floor antiques haven sell everything from art deco to mid-20th-century modern.
✚ Off map to north
⊠ 6130 N Broadway Avenue
☎ 773/743–5444 ⓠ Red line: Granville ⬛ 136

CHRISTA'S LTD

Stuffed with predominantly 18th- and 19th-century fare, including tables, bureaux, cabinets, crystalware, mirrors, lamps, clocks and much more from Europe and the US.
✚ G5 ⊠ 217 W Illinois Street
☎ 312/222–2520 ⓠ Red line: Grand ⬛ 65

JAY ROBERT'S ANTIQUE WAREHOUSE

You'll find everything from clocks to fireplaces among the antiques and junk that fill 50,000sq ft (4,645sq m) of floor space here.
✚ G5 ⊠ 149 W Kinzie Street
☎ 312/222–0167 ⓠ Brown, Purple lines: Merchandise Mart ⬛ 36, 62

LINCOLN ANTIQUE MALL

Everything that could ever be considered an antique, and quite a lot that could never be, can be found amid these cluttered stalls.
✚ Off map to north ⊠ 3141 N Lincoln Avenue
☎ 773/244–1440 ⓠ Brown line: Paulina ⬛ 9, 11, 77

POSTER PLUS

Historic posters, mostly celebrating landmarks in Chicago and US history, though many are attractive reprints rather than originals.
✚ H7 ⊠ 200 S Michigan Avenue ☎ 800/659–1905
ⓠ Brown, Orange lines: Adams ⬛ 3, 4, 6, 38

R. H. LOVE GALLERIES

For decades Chicago's leading purveyor of fine American paintings and prints; even if the purchase of an original is beyond your means, turn uo to admire the displays and frequent exhibitions.
✚ H5 ⊠ 2nd floor, 645 N Michigan Avenue
☎ 800/437–7568 ⓠ Red line: Grand ⬛ 3, 11, 125, 145, 146, 147, 151

STEVE STARR STUDIOS

A wonderful selection of original art-deco paraphernalia, ranging from silver cigarette cases to chrome cocktail shakers.
✚ E1 ⊠ 2779 N Lincoln Avenue ☎ 773/525–6530
ⓠ Brown line: Diversey ⬛ 11, 76

VINTAGE POSTERS INTERNATIONAL

Stylish posters from the US and Europe dating from the 1880s, plus a diverse selection of French decorative items of the belle époque.
✚ G3 ⊠ 1551 N Wells Street
☎ 312/951–6681 ⓠ Brown line: Sedgwick ⬛ 135, 156

Books

ABRAHAM LINCOLN BOOK SHOP

Autographs, rare manuscripts, historic pamphlets and, of course, books by or about Abraham Lincoln.

🔢 G5 ✉ 357 W Chicago Avenue ☎ 312/944–3085 🚇 Brownor Red lines: Chicago 🚌 11, 66, 156

AFTER-WORDS

New titles on most subjects, but leaning towards less-than-mainstream fiction, politics and history; plus a gigantic stock of used books on all subjects.

🔢 G5 ✉ 23 E Illinois Street ☎ 312/464–1110 🚇 Red line: Grand 🚌 22, 29, 36

BARBARA'S BOOKSTORE

Old, new and otherwise hard-to-find literature, plus political and contemporary lifestyle titles.

🔢 G3 ✉ 1350 N Wells Street ☎ 312/642–5044 🚇 Brown line: Sedgwick; Red line: Clark/Division 🚌 11, 156

BOOKSAMILLION

There could well be a million books, mostly mainstream titles on diverse subjects, amid these tightly stacked shelves.

🔢 G6 ✉ 144 S Clark Street ☎ 312/857–0613 🚇 Blue or Red lines: Washington 🚌 22, 24

CHICAGO ARCHITECTURE FOUNDATION

Exemplary source of books on architecture.

🔢 H7 ✉ 224 S Michigan Avenue ☎ 312/922–3432 🚇 Brown, Orange lines: Adams 🚌 3, 4, 6, 38

CHICAGO RARE BOOK CENTER

Intriguing assortment of first editions and other volumes that span fiction, history, the arts, travel and many more subjects. Also has a browse-worthy stock of historic maps and photos of Chicago in poster form.

🔢 G4 ✉ 56 W Maple Street ☎ 312/988–7246 🚇 Red line: Chicago 🚌 22

57TH STREET BOOKS

Hyde Park institution, with both new and used volumes. Toys are provided for children of browsing parents.

🔢 Off map to south ✉ 1301 E 57th Street ☎ 773/684–1300 🚇 Red line: Garfield 🚇 55th, 56th, 57th Street 🚌 1, 4, 28, 51

OCCULT BOOSTORE

On the third floor of the Flat Iron Arts Building lurks this repository of new, used and rare works covering magic, tarot, astrology and more.

🔢 C/D3 ✉ 1579 N Milwaukee Avenue ☎ 773/292–0995 🚇 Blue line: Damen 🚌 56

QUIMBY'S BOOKSTORE

Alternative bookstore selling every title imaginable.

🔢 D3 ✉ 1854 W North Avenue ☎ 773/342–0910 🚇 Blue line: Damen 🚌 56

RAND MCNALLY MAP STORE

Atlases, regional and city street maps; guidebooks.

🔢 H5 ✉ 444 N Michigan Avenue ☎ 312/321–1751 🚇 Red line: Grand 🚌 3, 11, 145, 146, 147, 151

PRINTER'S ROW BOOKSHOPS

A cluster of noteworthy bookstores lies just south of the Loop in Printer's Row (► 53). Prairie Avenue Bookshop (✉ 418 S Wabash Avenue) stocks seemingly every tome on architecture and town planning ever published. Powell's Bookstore (✉ 828 S Wabash Avenue) carries second-hand books on all subjects.

NATIONAL CHAINS

The Diversey branch of Barnes & Noble (✉ 659 W Diversey Parkway ☎ 773/871–9004 🚇 Brown line: Diversey 🚌 22, 36, 76) is a superstore, with shelf after shelf of general titles, newspapers and magazines, in an atmosphere conducive to browsing. Borders Books & Music (✉ 830 N Michigan Avenue ☎ 312/573–0564 🚇 Red line: Chicago 🚌 145, 146, 147, 151) has a comparably huge selection. Both have cafés.

Discount Shops & Outlets

LONG-DISTANCE DISCOUNT SHOPPING

Two major outlet malls on the edge of the Chicago area are worth the trip. An hour or so's journey west finds Gurnee Mills (☎ 800/937–7467), whose 200-plus stores are easily combined with a trip to Six Flags Great America (► 20). An hour south in Michigan City, Indiana, is Lighthouse Place (☎ 219/879–6506), another extensive group of factory retail outlets.

BROWN ELEPHANT

Immensely browsable stock of clothing for men and women, furniture, ornaments, books and other items.
✚ Off map to north
✉ 3651 N Halsted Street
☎ 773/549–5943 🚇 Brown or Red lines: Belmont 🚌 152

CRATE & BARREL OUTLET

A small factory outlet with hefty discounts on the admirable Crate & Barrel houseware and furniture.
✚ F3 ✉ 800 W North Avenue
☎ 312/787–4775 🚇 Brown line: Sedgwick

CYTHNIA'S CONSIGNMENTS

A massive stock of designer wear at eye-watering discounts, including a large stock of bridal gowns.
✚ D2 ✉ 2218 N Clybourne Avenue ☎ 773/248–7714
🚇 Brown or Red lines: Fullerton
🚌 56

DESIGNER RESALE

Names such as Armani and Chanel are among the designer labels offered second-hand in this chic womenswear boutique.
✚ G5 ✉ 658 N Dearborn Street ☎ 312/587–3312
🚇 Red line: Grand 🚌 22

DSW SHOE WAREHOUSE

Whether in need of designer shoes for a top night out or simply solid footwear, this long established outlet is the place to find them.
✚ Off Map to north
✉ 3100 N Clark Street

☎ 773/975–7182 🚇 Brown or Red lines: Belmont 🚌 22, 36

FILENE'S BASEMENT

Formidably large stock— spread over several floors—of designer clothing and accessories for men and women at 30 to 60 percent off retail prices.
✚ H4 ✉ 830 N Michigan Avenue ☎ 312/482–8918
🚇 Red line: Chicago 🚌 145, 146, 147, 151
Also at:
✚ G6 ✉ 1 N State Street

GAP FACTORY OUTLET

Big discounts on Gap and Banana Republic stock.
✚ B/C2 ✉ 2778 N Milwaukee Avenue ☎ 773/252–0594
🚇 Blue line: Western

MCSHANE'S EXCHANGE

The latest designer clothing for women, barely worn and temptingly priced.
✚ F2 ✉ 1141 W Webster Avenue ☎ 773/525–0211
🚇 Brown line: Armitage 🚌 73

RECYCLE IT

Row after row of mid-range designer clothing for men and women fills this aircraft-hanger-like space—at very affordable prices.
✚ C3 ✉ 1474 N Milwaukee Avenue ☎ 773/645–1900
🚇 Blue line: Damen 🚌 56

THE SECOND CHILD

Designer children's clothes, furnishings and toys, second-hand but in excellent condition.
✚ E2 ✉ 954 W Armitage Avenue ☎ 773/883–0880
🚇 Brown line: Armitage 🚌 73

Miscellaneous

AMERICAN GIRL PLACE

A landmark for girls who love the eponymous dolls. Everything here is American Girl—clothes, books, stage shows, lessons in etiquette, afternoon tea and lots more. For some, a shrine.
✚ G5 ✉ 111 E Chicago Avenue ☎ 877/AG–PLACE or 312/943–9400 🚇 Red line: Chicago 🚌 11, 66

ANCIENT ECHOES

Intriguing stash of handicrafted jewelry, decorative arts and funishings, from earrings and rings to tabletops and tiles.
✚ E2 ✉ 1022A W Armitage Avenue ☎ 800/292–0929 🚇 Brown or Red lines: Armitage 🚌 73

CHICAGO MUSIC MART

Pianos, ocarinas and Indian *tablas* are among the instruments you can find at this gathering of music retailers. Or look for the musically themed sweets.
✚ H7 ✉ 333 S State Street ☎ 312/362–6700 🚇 Blue, Red lines: Jackson 🚌 1, 7, 60, 126, 145, 146, 147, 151

JAZZ RECORD MART

Mainstream releases and cult rarities are among its thousands of CDs, records and tapes.
✚ G5 ✉ 444 N Wabash Avenue ☎ 312/222–1467 🚇 Red line: Grand 🚌 22, 29, 36

NIKE TOWN

Even if you couldn't care less about Nike sports-wear, a visit to this pulsating, themed, tri-level store—complete with aquarium—is a must.
✚ H5 ✉ 669 N Michigan Avenue ☎ 312/642–6363 🚇 Red line: Chicago 🚌 145, 146, 147, 151

THE SAVVY TRAVELER

Everything travelers might need—from money belts to guidebooks.
✚ H7 ✉ 310 S Michigan Avenue ☎ 312/913–9800 🚇 Brown, Orange lines: Adams 🚌 3, 4, 6, 38

SONY GALLERY OF CONSUMER ELECTRONICS

Despite the museum-like displays, this really is a shop for showcasing Sony's latest items. Slim-screen computers, memory sticks, wide-screen TVs and Playstations are all here.
✚ H4 ✉ 633 N Michigan Avenue ☎ 312/943–3334 🚇 Red line: Chicago 🚌 145, 146, 147, 151

SPORTSWORLD

Appropriately neighboring Wrigley Field, this stocks the biggest array of Chicago Cubs clothing imaginable, plus wearable souvenirs of Wrigley Field itself.
✚ Off map to north ✉ 3555 N Clark Street ☎ 773/472–7701 🚇 Red line: Addison 🚌 22, 152

TOWER RECORDS

Every record or CD ever released in any musical category (it seems), plus books and videos.
✚ G2 ✉ 2301 N Clark Street ☎ 773/477–5994 🚇 Brown, Red lines: Fullerton 🚌 22, 36

CIGARS AND MORE

Chicago's several shops for discerning smokers offer quality hand-rolled cigars and, usually, imported cigarettes and smokers' accessories. Three of the best are Up and Down Tobacco (✉ 1550 Wells Street), Blue Havana (✉ 46 E Oak Street) and Little Havana (✉ 6 W Maple Street and at Navy Pier, ➤ 46).

Blues & Jazz Spots

GRANT PARK'S BLUES AND JAZZ

Each June and September the Petrillo Music Shell in Grant Park (➤ 41) is the stage for blues and jazz festivals respectively, which draw top international names as well as the city's greats in both fields. The performers are greeted by tens of thousands of their admirers, who arrive with blankets and picnic supplies to enjoy the free music.

ANDY'S JAZZ CLUB

Popular and unpretentious jazz venue that earns its keep by staging commendable sets on weekday lunchtimes, as well as early and mid-evening shows.

H5 ✉ 11 E Hubbard Street ☎ 312/642–6805 🚇 Red line: Grand 🚌 29, 36

BE-BOP CAFÉ

Listen to be-bop and other jazz while tucking into jambalaya, barbecued ribs and other cajun dishes. Popular among music fans and tourists alike.

J/K5 ✉ Navy Pier, 600 E Grand Avenue ☎ 312/595–5299 🚌 29, 55, 65, 66

BLUE CHICAGO

Comfortable, homey blues club, showcasing home-grown musical talent.

G5 ✉ 736 N Clark Street ☎ 312/642–6261 🚇 Red line: Chicago 🚌 22, 36

BUDDY GUY'S LEGENDS

Co-owner and famed blues guitarist Buddy Guy presents outstanding blues acts, including internationally known names and local rising stars.

H7 ✉ 754 S Wabash Avenue ☎ 312/427–0333 🚇 Red line: Harrison 🚌 12

GREEN MILL

The jazz here is always good, sometimes brilliant. On Sunday nights, poets take to the stage for competitive poetry reading—more entertaining than you might think. Well north of the city in an unfashionable area, but worth the journey.

F1 ✉ 4802 N Broadway ☎ 773/878–5552 🚇 Brown line: Diversey 🚌 136

HOUSE OF BLUES

Blues and rock from around the city, the country and the world every night of the week. The smaller Back Porch stage has blues nightly, and is open at lunch for more of the same.

G5 ✉ 329 N Dearborn Street ☎ 312/923–2000 🚇 Red line: Grand 🚌 22, 36, 62

JAZZ SHOWCASE

Photos of jazz legends decorate this historic joint, and big names in contemporary jazz play here. Bring the kids to the Sunday matinee performances.

G5 ✉ 59 W Grand Avenue ☎ 312/670–2473 🚇 Red line: Grand 🚌 22, 65

KINGSTON MINES

Likeably medium-sized venue with live nightly blues on two stages.

Off map to north ✉ 2548 N Halsted Street ☎ 773/477–4646 🚇 Brown, Red lines: Fullerton 🚌 8

LEES UNLEADED BLUES

The reward for the lengthy journey from the heart of the city is this atmospheric South Side jazz and blues venue, mainly featuring talented local acts.

Off map to south ✉ 7401 S Chicago Avenue ☎ 773/493–3477 🚌 30

Comedy, Folk, Rock & Reggae Spots

BEAT KITCHEN
Smallish venue that makes a good setting for folk and rock acts, predominantly from around Chicago.
➕ Off map to north ✉ 2100 W Belmont Avenue ☎ 773/281–4444 🚇 Brown, Red lines: Belmont 🚌 22

CUBBY BEAR LOUNGE
Its location opposite Wrigley Field makes this sports bar a favorite spot for post-Cub games. Live music spans rock, country, and blues. Dancing and beer.
➕ Off map to north ✉ 1059 W Addison Street ☎ 773/327–1662 🚇 Brown line: Addison 🚌 22, 152

DOUBLE DOOR
In the heart of fashionable Wicker Park and well-established as the city's best mid-sized venue for rock and pop acts spanning the musical spectrum.
➕ D3 ✉ 1572 N Milwaukee Avenue ☎ 773/489–3190 🚇 Blue line: Damen 🚌 56

ELBO ROOM
Innovative two-floored venue for live alternative rock, often featuring hot new acts, poetry readings and comedy.
➕ Off map to north ✉ 2871 N Lincoln Avenue ☎ 773/549–5549 🚇 Brown line: Diversey 🚌 11

HOT HOUSE
Trendy, warehouse-like spot in South Loop area, with eclectic music and an arty crowd.
➕ H7 ✉ 31 W Balbo Drive ☎ 312/362–9707 🚇 Red line: Harrison 🚌 6, 146

IMPROVOLYMPIC
House comedians perform improvized sketches and entire musicals based on audience suggestions.
➕ Off map to north ✉ 3541 N Clark Street ☎ 773/880–0199 🚇 Brown, Red lines: Belmont 🚌 22, 156

METRO
The city's major mid-sized venue for live rock, with ample space for dancing and plentiful seating with good views. Other levels have a nightclub and coffee bar.
➕ Off map to north ✉ 3730 N Clark Street ☎ 773/549–0203 🚇 Brown line: Addison 🚌 22, 152

PARK WEST
Intimate size and strong acoustics make this the ideal place for non-earsplitting music, be it folk, jazz, rock or something else in the eclectic itinerary.
➕ F2 ✉ 322 W Armitage Avenue ☎ 773/929–5959 🚇 Brown or Red lines: Armitage 🚌 23, 72

THE WILD HARE
Top-notch live reggae and other Caribbean and African sounds in the heart of Wrigleyville.
➕ Off map to north ✉ 3530 N Clark Street ☎ 773/327–4273 🚇 Brown line: Addison 🚌 22, 152

ZANIES
Small, enjoyable comedy club, featuring rising local stars as well as better-known names.
➕ G3 ✉ 1548 N Wells Street ☎ 312/337–4027 🚇 Brown line: Sedgwick 🚌 11, 156

CAN YOU CROON IN TUNE

Karaoke supplies plenty of laughs as long as you have the key ingredient: a lively group that isn't afraid to embarrass itself by singing in public with a machine that serves up the words and music. If you're in the "Windy City" on a Tuesday, head over to the predominantly gay Circuit (✉ 3641 N Halsted ☎ 773/325–2233). On Thursdays, try Joe's Bar (✉ 940 W Weed Street ☎ 312/337–3486), where backing comes from a live band. Or you might visit Original Mother's (✉ 26 W Division Street ☎ 312/642–7251), also familiar as the watering hole patronized by Rob Lowe and Demi Moore in the film *About Last Night*.

Classical Music, Theater & the Performing Arts

RAVINIA FESTIVAL

From mid-June to Labor Day, the northern suburb of Highland Park plays host to the Ravinia Festival. The summer home of the Chicago Symphony Orchestra, Ravinia also stages rock and jazz concerts, dance events and other cultural activities. Chartered buses ferry festival-goers the 25 miles (40km) from central Chicago; you can also get there by commuter train. For further details ☎ 847/433–8819; www.ravinia.org

AUDITORIUM THEATER

Designed by the revered Adler & Sullivan, the marvelously renovated Auditorium Building was the world's heaviest structure when completed in 1889. Excellent acoustics and good sightlines make it a fine venue for dance, music and drama productions.

✚ H7 ✉ 50 E Congress Parkway ☎ 312/922–2110 🚇 Red line: Harrison 🚌 6, 145, 146, 147, 151

CHICAGO CENTER FOR THE PERFORMING ARTS

An expanding and well-equipped performance art and education complex staging diverse drama and music in its 350-seat main hall, as well as other events.

✚ F7 ✉ 777 N Green Street ☎ 312/327–2000 🚇 Blue line: Chicago 🚌 8, 66

CHICAGO SHAKESPEARE THEATER ON NAVY PIER

A 500-seat auditorium raised at a cost of $24 million makes a splendid setting for the works of the Bard; the performances are preceded by a half-hour lecture on the plays and discussions by the actors on their roles.

✚ J/K5 ✉ 600 E Grand Avenue ☎ 312/596–5600 🚇 Red line: Grand 🚌 29, 56, 65, 66

CHICAGO THEATER COMPANY

This African-American company stages some of the city's best contemporary productions at theaters around town. The repertoire mixes original material with adaptations.

✚ Off map to south ✉ 500 E 67th Street ☎ 773/493–0901 🚌 3

CIVIC OPERA HOUSE

The fine Lyric Opera of Chicago company performs from mid-September to early February at this art-deco auditorium (which is also one of the main dance venues). Seats are sometimes available at the box office on the day of performance.

✚ G6 ✉ 20 N Wacker Drive ☎ 312/419–0033 🚇 Brown, Orange lines: Madison/Wells 🚌 129

DANCE CENTER OF COLUMBIA COLLEGE

The 272-seat theater makes an intimate setting for productions by the Columbia dance college students; some feature internationally known artists.

✚ H8 ✉ 1306 S Michigan Avenue ☎ 312/344–8300 🚇 Brown, Orange, Red lines: Roosevelt 🚌 1, 3, 4

FORD CENTER FOR THE PERFORMING ARTS/ ORIENTAL THEATER

Still called the Oriental by locals, this ornate, 2,180-seat theater reopened in 1998 after a painstaking restoration. The North Loop theater presents first-rate shows in its top-notch performance space.

✚ H6 ✉ 24 W Randolph Street ☎ 312/902–1400

🅰 Red, Brown, Green, Orange
lines: Lake 🚌 156

GOODMAN THEATER

Adjoining the Art
Institute of Chicago
(► 40), the Goodman
hosts some of the best
drama in the city,
including both classics
and cutting-edge
contemporary
productions. The latter
are often staged in the
smaller of the building's
two auditoriums.
➕ G6 ✉ 170 N Dearborn
Street ☎ 312/443–3800
🅰 Blue line: Washington
🚌 22, 24, 36, 62

NOBLE FOOL

Spoofs, parodies and
other comedic fare are
the main source of the
resident company at this
160-seat venue.
➕ G6 ✉ 16 W Randolph
Street ☎ 312/726–1156
🅰 Red line: Washington; Brown
and Green lines Randolph
🚌 15, 36, 44, 146, 151

SECOND CITY

Biting satire and
inspired improvization
have long been the
stock-in-trade here, and
they have been so
successful that a second
Second City theater now
offers a different show
simultaneously.
➕ G3 ✉ 1616 N Wells Street
☎ 773/337–3992 🅰 Brown
line: Sedgwick 🚌 11, 156

SHUBERT THEATER

Dating back to the 19th
century, the handsome
Shubert is a rare
reminder that theater
once thrived in the
Loop. Dance companies
perform here, though it

is not exclusively a
dance theater. It is best
known for its musicals.
➕ G6 ✉ 22 W Monroe Street
☎ 312/977–1701 🅰 Brown,
Orange lines: Madison/Wells

STEPPENWOLF THEATER

Home of the enor-
mously successful and
influential Steppenwolf
repertory company,
founded in 1976, and
still a premier venue for
the best of Off-Loop
theater. The theater has
a 900-seat main hall and
a smaller space for
experimental drama.
➕ F3 ✉ 1650 N Halsted
Street ☎ 312/335–3830
🅰 Red line: North/Clybourn
🚌 8, 72

SYMPHONY CENTER

From September to May
the renowned Chicago
Symphony Orchestra
(CSO) is in residence in
this sumptuous Greek
Revival hall, built in
1904. Tickets are sold
early, but some may be
available on the day of
performance. The Civic
Orchestra of Chicago, a
training orchestra that
often gives free concerts,
appears here and there is
an annual jazz series.
➕ H7 ✉ 220 S Michigan
Avenue ☎ 312/294–3000
🅰 Brown, Orange lines: Adams
🚌 1, 3, 4, 6, 7, 38, 60

VICTORY GARDENS THEATER

Showcasing works of
aspiring Chicago
playwrights since 1974.
➕ F2 ✉ 2257 N Lincoln
Avenue ☎ 773/871–3000
🅰 Brown, Red lines: Fullerton
🚌 11

HALF-PRICE THEATER TICKETS

Hot Tix (✉ 108 N State Street
or Chicago Place, 700 N
Michigan Avenue) offers half-
price tickets for many of the
day's theater events. A
recorded message
(☎ 312/977–1755) and
website (www.hottix.org) lists
the day's performances. Full-
price advance tickets are also
available from Hot Tix, as well
as from another agency,
Ticketmaster
(☎ 312/559–1212).

COMEDY SHOWS

Two comedy shows have been
entertaining Chicago theater-
goers for years. *Tony 'n' Tina's
Wedding* (✉ 230 W North
Avenue ☎ 312/664–8844),
which started out in New York,
re-creates an Italian-American
wedding; the performers
mingle with the audience ("the
guests"). Meanwhile, *Late Nite
Catechism* (✉ Royal George
Theater, 1641 N Halsted
☎ 312/988–9000) is a one-
woman-show taking place on
Wednesday, Friday, Saturday
and Sunday in which a nun
recounts her American-
Catholic upbringing, with
audience participation.

Nightclubs

NIGHTCLUB NEWS

The most general source is the Friday edition of the *Chicago Tribune* and its Metromix website (www.metromix.com). Inside info on the latest clubs, as well as the nightlife scene in general, can be found in the pages of the weekly *Chicago Reader* and *New City*, both free of charge, and on their websites.

BERLIN

This big and immensely popular gay and lesbian nightspot puts on regular themed nights. It's packed to bursting on Fridays and Saturdays.

✚ Off map to north ✉ 954 W Belmont Avenue ☎ 773/348–4975 🚇 Brown, Red lines: Belmont 🚌 77

BIOLOGY BAR

Three bars and a dance floor—9,000sq ft (836sq m) pulsate with Latin and salsa, and lots more.

✚ F3 ✉ 1520 N Fremont Street ☎ 312/397–0580 🚇 Red line: North/Clybourn 🚌 8

CROBAR

The city's leading nightspot for trance, house and techno DJs; the place is packed on the weekend. Usually closed Monday and Tuesday.

✚ F5 ✉ 1543 N Kingsbury Street ☎ 312/266–1900 🚇 Red line: North/Clybourn 🚌 37, 125

DRINK

A riotous restaurant and bar in the former meatpacking district that later becomes a dance venue with throbbing live music. This spot is popular with people who work the nearby financial institutions.

✚ F6 ✉ 702 W Fulton Street ☎ 312/733–7800 🚌 56

EXCALIBUR

This complex of billiards, pinball, video games, discos and a restaurant is incongruously set in a 19th-century pseudo-Gothic castle, a sturdy granite structure built in the 1890s for the Chicago Historical Society. A favorite with twenty-somethings.

✚ G5 ✉ 632 N Dearborn Street ☎ 312/266–1944 🚇 Red line: Grand 🚌 22

NEO

An ultra-cool crowd laps up sounds ranging from industrial dance and techno to slightly more mainstream music. By city nightlife standards, this is an old-timer.

✚ G2 ✉ 2350 N Clark Street ☎ 773/528–2622 🚇 Brown, Red lines: Fullerton 🚌 22, 36

SPY BAR

Patrons dress in swanky club gear to edge past the bouncers, then sip Martinis before grooving to house music—the Spy Bar specialty. Sink into a velvet couch when you need a breather. Entrance through alleyway.

✚ G5 ✉ 646 N Franklin Street ☎ 312/587–8779 🚇 Brown line: Chicago 🚌 37

SYN

Futuristic/minimalist décor with a hint of decadence sets the tone for one of the city's newest and most upscale nightspots; the first choice for champagne-sipping clubbers.

✚ H4 ✉ 1009 N Rush Street ☎ 312/664–1001 🚇 Red line: Chicago 🚌 36

Bars

BILLY GOAT TAVERN
This below-street-level, unpretentious watering hole is a favorite among local journalists.
🏛 H5 ✉ 430 N Michigan Avenue ☎ 312/222–1525 Ⓡ Red line: Grand 🚌 145, 146, 147, 151

DELILAH'S
Offers a vast array of microbrewed beers, and an equally diverse range of whiskies, to a music-oriented crowd; drinking is aided by an eclectic DJ and regular live bands.
🏛 Off map to north ✉ 2771 N Lincoln Avenue ☎ 773/472–2771 Ⓡ Brown and Red lines: Diversey 🚌 11

DRU'S
Tucked away in Chinatown in this stylish bar-cum-club-cum-eatery, boasting a well-stocked bar and a hip clientele.
🏛 G9 ✉ 2101 S China Place ☎ 312/567–9349 Ⓡ Red line: Cermak/Chinatown 🚌 24

GAMEKEEPERS TAVERN & GRILL
A rowdy sports bar packed with televisions and raucous, twenty-something drinkers.
🏛 G2 ✉ 1971 N Lincoln Avenue ☎ 773/549–0400 Ⓡ Brown line: Armitage 🚌 11

HARRY CARAY'S
Created and named after the legendary baseball broadcaster who died in 1998, this sports bar is packed with baseball memorabilia. It's a great place to be after a Cubs win, and the Italian food is good.
🏛 G5 ✉ 33 W Kinzie Street ☎ 312/828–0966 Ⓡ Red line: Grand 🚌 62

KAZ BAR
Attempts to re-create Morocco in Chicago are rare and this gloriously kitsch rendition of the Kasbah is worth a look. If the plush sofas fail to appeal, sip your cocktail inside a tent.
🏛 G5 ✉ House of Blues Hotel, 333 N Dearborn Street ☎ 312/245–0333 Ⓡ Red line: Grand 🚌 22, 36, 62

SHEFFIELD'S WINE & BEER
On a sunny day, head for the patio bar to sample the selection of microbrews, most made on the premises.
🏛 Off map to north ✉ 3258 N Sheffield Avenue ☎ 773/281–4989 Ⓡ Brown, Red lines: Belmont 🚌 9, 77

TASTING ROOM
Great assortment of wines, liquors and more in a cozy, brick-and-wood setting.
🏛 E6 ✉ 1415 W Randolph Street ☎ 312/942–1313 Ⓡ Green line: Ashland 🚌 20

WEBSTER WINE BAR
As its name suggests, wine is the order of the day; a good selection is served in tranquil surroundings that extend outdoors during the summer.
🏛 E2 ✉ 1480 W Webster Avenue ☎ 773/868–0608 Ⓡ Brown or Red lines: Fullerton 🚌 74

LIQUOR LAWS
Some bars serve liquor until 2am every night except Saturday, when they may do so until 3am on Sunday morning. Others continue serving until 4am (5am on Sunday mornings). The drinking age is 21, and stores may not sell liquor before noon on Sundays.

Luxury Hotels

PRICES

Expect to pay the following prices per night for a double room:

Luxury – more than $200
Mid-Range – $120–$200
Budget – up to $120
Hostels – $15 per person

Many Chicago hotels offer weekend discounts, typically reducing the above prices by 20 to 40 percent.

CHICAGO HILTON & TOWERS

More than 1,600 rooms, a pervasive sense of grandeur and the city's largest hotel health club.
✚ H7 ✉ 720 S Michigan Avenue ☎ 800/HILTONS or 312/922–4400; fax 312/922–5240; www.chicagohilton.com 🚇 Red line: Harrison 🚌 1, 3, 4, 6, 146

THE DRAKE

Modeled on an Italian Renaissance palace and opened in 1920, this is among Chicago's finest hotels. Some of the 537 rooms have lake views.
✚ H4 ✉ 140 E Walton Place ☎ 800/55–DRAKE or 312/787–2200; fax 312/787–1431; www.thedrakehotel.com 🚇 Red line: Chicago 🚌 145, 146, 147, 151

EMBASSY SUITES

385 suites in a good location for Michigan Avenue shopping and River North nightlife. Substantial buffet breakfast and a free evening cocktail party are included.
✚ G5 ✉ 600 N State Street ☎ 312/943–3800 or 800/EMBASSY; fax 312/943–7629; www.embassysuiteschicago.com 🚇 Red line: Grand 🚌 36

FAIRMONT HOTEL

Winning views over Grant Park, the city and the lake; the 672 rooms are comfortable and tasteful. Use of health club nextdoor.
✚ H6 ✉ 200 N Columbus Drive ☎ 800/257–2544 or 312/565–8000; fax 312/856–1030; www.fairmont.com/chicago 🚇 Brown, Orange lines: State, Lake 🚌 4

FOUR SEASONS

Excellent service and 343 traditional rooms. Rooftop running track.
✚ H4 ✉ 120 E Delaware Place ☎ 800/332–3442 or 312/280–8800; fax 312/280–1748; www.fourseasons.com/chicagofs 🚇 Red line: Chicago 🚌 145, 146, 147, 151

RENAISSANCE CHICAGO

The convenient Loop location and the 553 spacious, well-equipped rooms make this a good choice for business travelers.
✚ H6 ✉ 1 W Wacker Drive ☎ 888/236–2427 or 312/372–7200; fax 312/372–0093; www.renaissancemarriott.com/propertyPage/CHISR 🚇 Red line: Lake, State; Brown, Green lines: State 🚌 2, 10, 11, 44

SUTTON PLACE

In a strikingly modern exterior amid Gold Coast brownstones, 246 comfortable rooms offer hi-speed internet access, climate control and umbrellas for rainy days.
✚ H4 ✉ 21 E Bellevue Place ☎ 312/266–2100 or 800/606–8188; fax 312/266–2103; www.suttonplace.com 🚇 Red line: Clarke/Division 🚌 Any N Michgan Avenue

THE WHITEHALL

First opened in the 1920s, this 221-room hotel now has English-style furnishings, and two-line phone and fax machines.
✚ H4 ✉ 105 E Delaware Place ☎ 800/948–4255 or 312/944–6300; fax 312/944–8552; www.thewhitehallhotel.com 🚇 Red line: Chicago 🚌 145, 146, 147, 151

Mid-Range Hotels

THE ALLEGRO

The 483 rooms are easily the best-priced in the Loop.

🚇 G6 ✉ 171 W Randolph Street ☎ 866/672–6143 or 312/236–0123; fax 312/236–3440; www.allegrochicago.com 🚉 Brown, Orange lines: Randolph/Wells 🚌 37

THE BURNHAM

Creative use of the historic Reliance Building (➤ 56) has yielded 141 comfortable if slightly cramped rooms. The Loop location is inspiring.

🚇 H6 ✉ 1 W Washington Street ☎ 312/782–1111 or 866/690–1986–9712; fax 312/783–0899; www.burnhamhotel.com 🚉 Blue, Red lines: Washington 🚌 147, 151

CITY SUITES HOTEL

Most of the 45 rooms are suites—and good value. A lively shopping and nightlife strip is on the doorstep.

🚇 Off map to north ✉ 933 W Belmont Avenue ☎ 773/404–3400 or 800/CITY–108; fax 773/404–3405; www.cityinns.com/index/citysuites.html 🚉 Brown, Red lines: Belmont 🚌 77

THE CLARIDGE

Very comfortable and well-sited on an Old Town residential street close to the Magnificent Mile. Mahogany furniture conceals internet access in all of the 56 rooms and suites.

🚇 G3 ✉ 1244 N Dearborn Parkway ☎ 312/787–4980 or 800/245–1258; fax 312/266–0978; www.claridgehotel.com 🚉 Red line: Clark/Division 🚌 37, 156

COURTYARD BY MARRIOTT

The 337 large, comfortable, well-priced rooms are designed for business travelers. The Loop is adjacent. Golf course nearby.

🚇 G5 ✉ 30 E Hubbard Street ☎ 800/228–9290 or 312/329–2500; fax 312/329–0293; www.marriott.com 🚉 Red line: Grand 🚌 36

OLD TOWN CHICAGO

Just four suites, sumptuously furnished in a manner befitting the retro art-deco style of this town house. In a peaceful residential street in the Old Town.

🚇 G3 ✉ 1442 N North Park Avenue ☎ 312/440–9268; fax 312/440–2378; www.oldtownchicago.com 🚉 Brown line: Sedgwick 🚌 72

THE RAPHAEL

Tremendous value in an otherwise costly district, just off the Magnificent Mile. Most of the 172 rooms are suites with their own refrigerators.

🚇 H4 ✉ 201 E Delaware Place ☎ 800/983–7870 or 312/943–5000; fax 312/943–9483; www.raphaelchicago.com/welcome.asp 🚉 Red line: Chicago 🚌 145, 146, 147, 151

TREMONT HOTEL

This elegant, 130-room, Tudor-style hotel is a stone's throw from Michigan Avenue shopping. Piano bar and fitness complex.

🚇 H4 ✉ 100 E Chestnut Street ☎ 312/751–1900 or 800/621–8133; fax 312/751–8691; www.tremontchicago.com/welcome.asp 🚉 Red line: Chicago 🚌 145, 146, 147, 151

BOOKING

Rooms can be reserved by phone, fax or mail; book as early as possible. A deposit (usually by credit card) equivalent to the nightly rate will ensure your room is held at least until 6pm; inform the hotel if you are arriving later. Credit card is the usual payment method; traveler's checks or cash can be used, but payment might then be expected in advance. The total charge will include the city's 14.9 percent sales and room tax.

Budget Accommodations

BED AND BREAKFAST

Bed-and-breakfasts offer an interesting alternative to hotels. They are typically Victorian homes fitted out in sumptuous style and filled with antiques. B&Bs span all price categories and are in many areas of Chicago, with a particularly strong concentration in Oak Park. The Bed & Breakfast Chicago agency (☎ 800/375–7084 or 312/640–1050; www.athomeinchicago.com) operates a reservation system; it handles properties that are usually centrally located.

BEST WESTERN RIVER NORTH

The 145 rooms are good value if unexciting. The plus points are a rooftop pool, exercise room, restaurant and close proximity to the nightspots and restaurants of River North.
✚ G5 ✉ 125 W Ohio Street ☎ 800/727–0800 or 312/467–0800; fax 312/467–1665; www.bestwestern.worldexecutive.com/diretory/usa/chicago/hotels/14112.htm 🚇 Red line: Grand 🚌 22

CASS HOTEL

Once past the forlorn lobby and the shabby downstairs bar you will find 180 clean rooms at a budget price within easy reach of the Magnificent Mile and River North. Also has free Wi-Fi internet access in its café and (paid for) internet access from a public kiosk in the lobby area.
✚ H5 ✉ 640 N Wabash Avenue ☎ 800/CASS–850 or 312/787–4030; fax 312/787–8544; www.casshotel.com 🚇 Red line: Grand 🚌 29, 65

DAYS INN LINCOLN PARK NORTH

A 133-room motel at the busy intersection of Broadway, Clark and Diversey, and a stone's throw from Wrigley Field. Price includes continental breakfast buffet.
✚ F1 ✉ 644 W Diversey Parkway ☎ 773/525–7010 or 888/LPNDAYS; fax 773/525–6998; www.lpndaysinn.com/index2.html 🚇 Brown line: Diversey 🚌 22

HOSTEL CHICAGO INTERNATIONAL

Also known as The J. Ira & Nicki Harris Family Hostel, this 1886 building on the southern edge of the Loop offers comfortable beds in 500 immaculate if spartan dorms that provide a perfect low-budget stay. Guests qualify for a range of discounts on local tours and other attractions.
✚ H7 ✉ 24 E Congress Parkway ☎ 312/360–0300; www.hichicago.org 🚇 Red line: Harrison 🚌 6, 146

OHIO HOUSE

This dependable, simple motel has 50 rooms and offers exceptional rates in a River North location. Adjoining coffee shop.
✚ G5 ✉ 600 N La Salle Street ☎ 312/943–6000; fax 312/943–6063 🚇 Red line: Grand 🚌 37, 41

WILLOWS HOTEL

55 great-value rooms on a residential street in Lake View, close to the lake, Lincoln Park and numerous bars and restaurants. The building dates from the 1920s and is full of character—the lobby is especially charming, with a fireplace and high windows.
✚ Off map to north ✉ 555 W Surf Street ☎ 773/528–8400 or 800/787–3108; www.cityinns.com/index/willows/html 🚇 Brown line: Diversey 🚌 36

CHICAGO
travel facts

ESSENTIAL FACTS

Customs regulations

- Duty-free allowances include 32fl oz alcoholic spirits or wine (no one under 21 may bring alcohol into the US), 200 cigarettes or 50 cigars, and up to $100-worth of gifts.
- Some medication bought over the counter abroad may be prescription-only in the US and may be confiscated. Bring a doctor's certificate for essential medication.
- It is forbidden to bring food, seeds and plants into the US.

Electricity

- The supply is 110 volts; 60 cycles AC current.
- US appliances use two-prong plugs. European appliances require an adaptor.

Etiquette

- Smoking is banned in all public buildings and transportation. It is also banned or restricted in many hotels and restaurants.
- Tipping is voluntary, but the following are usually expected: 15 percent-plus in restaurants; 15–20 percent for taxis; $1 per bag for a hotel porter.

Lavatories

- Most department stores, malls and hotel lobbies have adequate lavatories.

Money matters

- Most banks have ATMs, which accept credit cards registered in other countries that are linked to the Cirrus or Plus networks. Ensure your personal identification number is valid in the US: four- and six-figure numbers are usual.
- Credit cards are widely accepted.
- US dollar traveler's checks function like cash in most shops; $20 and $50 denominations are most useful. Seeking to exchange these (or foreign currency) at a bank can be difficult and commissions can be high.
- An 8.75 percent sales tax is added to marked retail prices, except on groceries and prescription drugs.

National holidays

- New Year's Day (1 Jan)
- Martin Luther King Day (third Mon in Jan)
- President's Day (third Mon in Feb)
- Memorial Day (last Mon in May)
- Independence Day (4 July)
- Labor Day (first Mon in Sep)
- Columbus Day (second Mon in Oct)
- Veteran's Day (11 Nov)
- Thanksgiving Day (fourth Thu in Nov)
- Christmas Day (25 Dec)

Opening hours

- Stores: Mon–Sat from 9 or 10 until 5 or 6. Most stores are also open Sun noon–5. Department stores and malls keep longer hours; bookshops may open in the evenings.
- Banks: Mon–Fri from 8 or 9 to 3, 4 or 5, with some branches open later once a week.

Solo visitors

- Solo visitors, including women, are not unusual.
- Women may encounter

unwanted attention and, after dark, should avoid being out alone when not in established nightlife areas. Wait for a cab inside a club or restaurant, or where staff can see you.

Student visitors
- An International Student Identity Card (ISIC) reduces admission to many museums and other attractions.
- Anyone aged under 21 is forbidden to buy or drink alcohol and may be denied admission to some nightclubs.

Tourist offices
- Visitor centers are inside the Chicago Water Tower ✉ 163 E Pearson Street ☎ 312/744–2400, at the Chicago Cultural Center ✉ 77 E Randolph Street ☎ 312/744–2400, and at Illinois Market Place ✉ Navy Pier, 700 E Grand Avenue. All are open daily but may close on holidays.

GETTING AROUND

- Chicago is served by a network of El (elevated railway) trains and buses.
- Using trains or buses at night can be dangerous.
- Metra commuter trains are best for visiting some areas.
- For information on the El and buses: Chicago Transit Authority ☎ 888/YOUR–CTA; Metra ☎ 312/322–6777 (🕐 Mon–Fri 8–5), otherwise 312/836–7000

The El
- Fare: $1.75. Transfer to a different line (or to a bus) within two hours: 25¢ (free within Loop). A second transfer within the same two

hours is free.
- Plastic transit cards are the simplest way to pay fares. Tokens ($13.50 for ten) and cash are the alternatives.
- Rechargable transit cards— available in any value from $1.50–$91—can also be used on buses, as can visitor passes valid for 1 day ($5), 2 days ($9), 3 days ($12) or 4 days ($18).
- Stations have fare booths or automatic ticket machines.
- Six color-coded lines run through the city and converge on the Loop.
- On weekdays 6am–7pm, trains on most lines stop only at alternate stations, plus all major stations. Check in advance whether you need to take the A or the B service.
- Most trains run 24 hours; frequency is reduced during weekends and late evenings.
- Some stations are closed at the weekend.

Buses
- Fare: $1.75. Transfer to a different route (or to the El) within two hours: 25¢. Second transfer as for the El.
- As for the El, plastic transit cards are the simplest way to pay fares. Tokens (as for the El) and cash (exact change only) are the alternatives.

Schedule and map information
- CTA maps showing El and bus routes are available from El station fare booths.
- Bus routes are shown at stops.

Taxis
- Fares are $1.90 plus $1.60 per mile and 50¢ each for more than one passenger.

- Hotel, restaurant and nightclub staff will order a taxi on request; or you can phone American United ☎ 312/248 7600; Checker ☎ 312/243 2537; Yellow ☎ 312/829 4222

MEDIA & COMMUNICATIONS

Telephones

- Public telephones are found in the street and in public buildings. Local calls cost 35¢.
- Calls from hotel rooms are usually more expensive than those from public phones.
- Many businesses have toll-free numbers, prefixed 800.
- Most US phones use touch-tone dialling, enabling callers to access extensions directly.
- To call Chicago from the UK dial 001 followed by the full number. To call the UK from Chicago dial 011 and omit the first zero from the area code.

Post offices

- Minimum charges for sending a postcard or letter overseas are 50¢ and 60¢ respectively.
- Main post office ✉ 433 W Harrison Street. To find the nearest post office, look in the phone book or ask at your hotel. Most open Mon–Fri 8.30–5, Sat 8.30–1 ☎ 312/654–3789

Newspapers and magazines

- Major daily newspapers are the *Chicago Tribune* and the tabloid *Chicago Sun-Times* (both have international, national and local stories).
- Best of several free weeklies is the *Chicago Reader*.
- Glossy monthly magazines such as *Chicago* reflect the interests of the well-heeled

Chicagoan. *Windy City Times* is pitched at gays and lesbians.
- Free magazines such as *Chicago Key*, found in hotel lobbies, are aimed at tourists.

International newsagents

- Overseas newspapers and magazines can be found at Barnes & Noble and Borders Books & Music stores (► 77).

Radio

- Classical: WFMT 98.7FM
- Country: WUSN 99.5FM
- Jazz: WNUA 95.5FM
- National Public Radio: WBEZ 91.5FM
- News: WBBM 780AM, WMAQ 670AM
- Rock: WCKG 105.9FM
- R&B: WGCI 107.5FM
- Talk radio and local sports: WGN 820AM

Television

- The main Chicago TV channels are 2 WBBM (CBS), 5 WMAQ (NBC), 7 WLS (ABC), 9 WGN (local WB affiliate), 11 WTTW (PBS), 32 WFLD (Fox).

EMERGENCIES

Sensible precautions

- By day, the Loop and major areas of interest to visitors are relatively safe. Some tourist sites involve journeys through unwelcoming areas; be especially wary if traveling through the South Side and Near West Side. Discuss your itinerary with hotel staff and heed their advice.
- After dark, stay in established nightlife areas. River North and River West, Rush and

Division streets, and Lake View/Wrigleyville are fairly safe if you use common-sense precautions. Public transportation is generally safe between these areas, but be cautious.

- Neighborhoods can change character within a few blocks. Stick to safe, busy streets.
- Carry shoulder bags strapped across your chest, and keep your wallet in your front trouser pocket or chest pocket. Keep your belongings within sight and within reach.
- Store valuables in your hotel's safe and never carry more money than you need.
- Lost traveler's checks are easy to replace—read the instructions when you buy them and keep the instructions handy (separate from the checks).
- Replacing a stolen passport is tricky and begins with a visit or phone call to your nearest consular office.
- Report any item stolen to the nearest police precinct (see the phone book). It is unlikely that stolen goods will be recovered but the police will fill in the forms your insurance company needs.

Lost property
- O'Hare International Airport ☎ 773/686–2201
- Lost in a cab ☎ 312/744–2900 or 312/744–6227
- The El and buses: Chicago Transit Authority ☎ 888/YOUR–CTA; Metra ☎ 312/322–6777 (🕐 Mon–Fri 8–5), or 312/836–7000

Medical treatment
- For doctors, ask hotel staff or the non-emergency

Medical Referral Service ☎ 312/670–2550
- In an emergency go to a hospital with a 24-hour emergency room, such as Northwestern Memorial Hospital ✉ 233 E Superior Street ☎ 312/926–2000
- The Chicago Dental Association ☎ 312/836–7300 will refer you to a dentist in your area.

Medicines
- Pharmacies are listed in *Yellow Pages*. Visitors from Europe will find many familiar medicines under unfamiliar names. Some drugs, available over the counter at home, are prescription only in the US.
- If you use medication bring a supply (but note the warning given in Customs Regulations, ► 90). If you intend to buy prescription drugs in the US, bring a note from your doctor.
- Late-night pharmacies in the city include Walgreen's ✉ 757 N Michigan Avenue ☎ 312/321–3622 🕐 24 hours. Osco Drug has a toll-free number ☎ 888/443–5701 giving the location of its nearest 24-hour branch.

Emergency telephone numbers
- Fire, police or ambulance ☎ 911 (no money required)
- Rape Crisis Hotline ☎ 888/293–2080

Consulates
- Germany ✉ 676 N Michigan Avenue, Suite 3200 ☎ 312/580–1199
- Ireland ✉ 400 N Michigan Avenue, Suite 911 ☎ 312/337–1868
- UK ✉ 400 N Michigan Avenue, Suite 1300 ☎ 312/346–1810

Index